Dear Marian,
Celebrate your artistic
journey and all your
successes.
Love,
Karlyn Holman
6/2002

# Searching for the
# Artist Within

ADS PHOTOGRAPHY

Karlyn Holman has had a studio/gallery since 1968 and enjoys being a full-time painter, gallery owner and workshop teacher. Karlyn has always lived by the shores of Lake Superior and has derived inspiration for her watercolor paintings from the beauty of that area, as well as from her travels around the world. Her paintings have been described as realism based on abstract structure, yet they remain experimental in nature. She has illustrated four children's picture books, one illustrated book and two instructional books on watercolor. She has taught on location in England, Italy, Norway, Sweden, Russia, Guatemala, Greece, France,

Portugal, the Yucatan, China, Hong Kong, Bangkok, Singapore, Ireland, Bulgaria and on three cruises in the Caribbean. Karlyn always knew she wanted to be an artist and pursued this dream through college, receiving an MA in Art from the University of Wisconsin. She taught art at the college level for ten years and currently teaches high-energy watercolor workshops around the world. Karlyn's enthusiastic and humorous teaching style makes beginners feel comfortable, yet challenges advanced students.

Karlyn and her husband, Gary, have three adult children and six grandchildren, and are both natives of Washburn, Wisconsin, a small village on the south shore of Lake Superior. Visit her on the web at www.karlynholman.com

*I would like to thank the following people:*

My mother and father, Lucille and Jack, who nurtured and encouraged me to become an artist.

The contributing artists who shared their inspiring words and artistic visions.

My publisher: John Teeter; my editor: Terri Wagner; and my graphic designer: Jan Esposito, for their invaluable help in making this book a reality.

Helen Bush, Bonnie Broitzman, Stella Canfield and the many other colleagues who made suggestions and shared their wisdom.

Bayfield Street Publishing, Inc.
116-1/2 East 5th Street
Washburn, Wisconsin 54891
715.373.1040
www.bayfieldstreet.com

10 9 8 7 6 5 4 3 2 1
Edited by Teresa Wagner and Jan Esposito
Designed by Jan Esposito, Printing Plus/Screen Line
Photography by Karlyn Holman and John Murphy, unless otherwise noted

Printed in Korea by Doosan Corporation

Library of Congress Control Number: 2002102589
ISBN 0-9670683-5-5 (alk. paper)  ISBN 0-9670683-7-1 (pbk.)

# Searching for the Artist Within

## Karlyn Holman

Bayfield Street Publishing, Inc.
Washburn, Wisconsin

# The color of courage

This book is dedicated to my friend Kim, an artist, art educator, art advocate and courageous person. After a long period of deliberation, Kim decided to become a full-time artist in 1996 and continued to perfect her own unique style. Kim courageously battled pancreatic cancer and died in January 2002. She had these words of inspiration to share.

## Kim Falk

### KEEPER OF DREAMS

"Follow your dreams, letting your heart lead you in your journey. Remember, the light comes from within and we create with our hearts not our hands.

"As an artist, I can represent life as only I see it, feel it and become it. To me, life is a search and a journey for inner peace, beauty and contentment. In my art I have found that sense. Creating my art is a burning need and passion for me. I have lived my dreams with no regrets. It takes courage and self-discipline to take that path, but the rewards are many, the lives you touch are endless, and the joy you receive is unimaginable.

"We as artists are the keepers of dreams: Dance with us the keepers of dreams, join our circle of creation. We are the souls of the past and the voices of the future, calling to you. Come; be drawn into our circle of light. We are the symphony of existence, storytellers all, exploring the nuances of life through all ages. Join us in our quest. We are the visionaries searching for answers to unknown questions. We are the guides, leading you to illumination all the while following our own path. Come; join us in our world. Let the songs of our art envelope you. Dance with us, the keepers of dreams."

"I think of my paintings as a slice of life, light and feelings to give you a sense of time and place. Each painting is a drama that is played and replayed."

Hide Away, Kim Falk

THE WEATHERED LOOK, Kim Falk

ANYONE HOME?, Kim Falk

*"My work explores the drama of high contrast. Most of my paintings are filled with lights and darks and sunlight and shadow. It is the contrast between the two that creates interest and excitement."*

SOUTHERN COMFORT, Kim Falk

Karlyn Holman

Karlyn Holman

# Table of Contents

Karlyn Holman

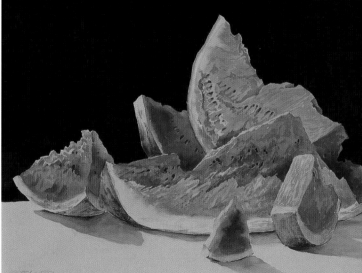

Frank Zeller

Karlyn Holman

# Introduction

*"Every child is an artist. The problem is how to remain an artist once he grows up."*
*Pablo Picasso*

Art is not something apart from our lives. Art is about love, adventure, meditation, visual therapy, humor and, most of all, a celebration of life. For as long as there has been documentation of human records, artists have conveyed their ideas and emotions through symbols and drawings. Art is who we are. Choosing to be an artist is more of an emotional choice than a physical choice. The act of creation is a way for people to share their observations and express their feelings.

As artists, we all see the world differently; this fact is really obvious when I paint on-location with my artist friends. Bonnie may interpret the scene using predominantly negative shapes, I usually paint in predominantly positive shapes, and my friend Mary enjoys making up shapes. These varying approaches demonstrate that your search for your personal expression began long before you picked up a brush. Every life experience, including the kind of nurturing and encouragement you may or may not have experienced, your self-confidence and your art experience all play a part in every painting you create. All the demands put on your life affect your art; all the challenges and joys filter down through your work. As you grow, your work will evolve. We each define our own reality in our paintings. We learn how to be an artist by looking and sharing and experiencing. Art usually starts with an infatuation and then grows into a passion that must be nurtured. Your desire and your search to gain information, skills and experience are the keys to becoming an artist. This search will constantly change as you grow in your skills. Much of the joy is in the search itself; one painting will lead to another. The more you know, the more you will realize there is more out there to know. Very few artists can rely solely on God-given talent. What it really takes is self-discipline and hard work.

**Painting is an endless search that never follows a straight path; it is an ongoing journey that can become a way of life.**
A willingness to keep searching will keep your work fresh and will foster growth in your interpretation. Your search can be focused on new ideas, special places, or it can go back to all the stored images in your memory. Your search can go in any direction—inward or outward. No two artists follow the same path or reach the same destination. I am still exploring my path and its many turns with no specific destination in sight.

Each artist has a different way of expressing his or her truth. The search to gain information, skills and experience is the key to becoming an artist.

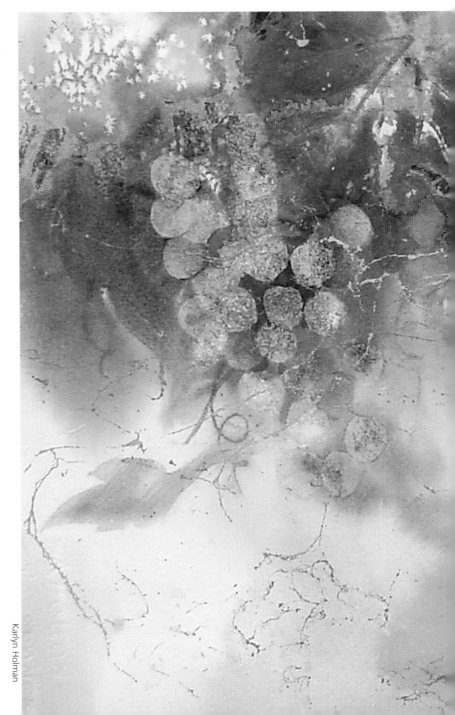

Karlyn Holman

This book shares many techniques that may challenge and inspire you to paint any subject and features the unique perspectives of over thirty artists who, in their own words, are willing to share their accomplishments.

Watercolor is unquestionably my primary media. The medium offers such extremes of interpretation, including everything from creating spontaneous wet-into-wet starts to focusing on precise detail. My early training included everything but watercolor, and when

I discovered the immediacy, transparency, excitement and challenge of watercolor, it completely captured my heart. Watercolor was the friend that welcomed me to adventure travel. It became my companion in my studio and at workshops, challenging me to experiment with new techniques, and actually, the medium has been my greatest teacher. I have an almost childlike enthusiasm for watercolor that never seems to fade. I feel so lucky to have chosen a profession I can share with you as you try new approaches and find success and confidence in your own search.

# CHAPTER ONE
# Searching for inspiration

*"Every artist dips his brush in his own soul and paints his own nature into his pictures."*

*Henry Ward Bucher*

Searching for inspiration is an ongoing endeavor driven by your desire and your commitment. Each artist has a different message carrying his or her truth. The spark of inspiration may come from dreams and fantasies or from a relationship with nature. Many artists are simply inspired by their celebration of everyday common objects. The subjects that inspire artists are as unique as the artists themselves.

When you become fully committed to your search, you need to make certain decisions. Every serious artist needs to set up a **studio** and find the **time** to paint. Your personal space must be tailored to meet your specific needs and should be filled with art materials, books and objects that inspire and motivate you to paint. Your studio provides a space for long, undisturbed periods of time to work, explore and experiment, which, in turn, allows you to grow in your artistic skills.

You need to challenge yourself to explore new vistas. The energy gained by painting or observing on location and experiencing the sights and sounds directly is totally different than the energy you experience working in your studio. Working on location permits you to gather information to store in your memory, to sketch and paint what you see, or to photograph subjects for future reference. Your mind and your visual resources work together with your hand and paintbrush to create a painting. Working with a live model or still life in your studio also provides a sense of immediacy because you have the actual subject in front of you. Whether you go on a travel adventure or simply step out into your back yard, working on location will expand your horizons. To become an artist is a lifelong search and an on-going process enriched by travel, life experiences and desire.

# Nature

One of the most powerful sources of inspiration is nature. When you take the time to immerse yourself in the natural world, you often recapture that wide-eyed delight that you experienced as a child. The shapes, changing light, abstract patterns, textures, smells and sounds all stimulate our senses and may evoke a different emotional response in each of us. You can use your mind's eye to remember the experience, you can get out your camera and try to capture the subject, or you can paint right on the scene.

Artists often notice subjects that other people easily overlook. Most of us have been trained to view nature as a panoramic postcard, and we miss the wealth of detail that makes up the whole. You can find subjects that other people easily overlook by using a more myopic point of view. For example, study the dried grasses peeking through a drift of snow or a clump of marsh marigolds growing in a ditch filled with water. Open up all your senses. When you learn to appreciate the intricacy of nature, you will discover a new world of subjects.

For example, one day after painting all morning on location in Hydra, Greece, I was sitting in a restaurant waiting for my lunch when these potted geraniums caught my eye. The plants were scraggly and obviously needed to be repotted, but something about the way the light danced on and around the flowers inspired me to take out my paper and start sketching. I had them sketched before lunch arrived, and after a delightful meal, I added the color and finished the painting.

Karlyn Holman

Karlyn Holman

# Nature as an inspirational teacher

Rather that pursue formal training at an art school, Greg chose to live with nature and experience first-hand its raw beauty. With the entire world as his teacher, he diligently observed, drew, painted, photographed and internalized nature's many moods. His dramatic use of light and his sensitive interpretation have earned him ten state conservation stamps. He was chosen as Artist of the Year for the Rocky Mountain Elk Foundation and has sold over 200,000 pieces of artwork for the Bradford Exchange. Greg has finished in the top ten finalists for nine years running in the Federal Duck Stamp competition.

*g. Alexander*

"We are all born with certain gifts, and if we choose, through dedication and passion, we can turn these gifts into a talent. I fell in love with drawing at a very early age. One day, I watched my as my father took a plain white sheet of paper and penciled in a beautiful drawing of two lions lying on a rock. My obsession with drawing and painting the outdoors and wildlife had begun.

"After high school, I enrolled in an art college. Instead of being impressed with the wide array of classes and techniques offered by the college, I felt like I was being drawn farther and farther away from my own personal artistic quest—wildlife art. After one semester of floundering, I walked into the Dean of Students' office and explained my feelings by showing him my portfolio. He looked at my work, paused for a moment and then said, 'This school is not for you Greg. You need to keep going on your own, teach yourself as you have been with your reference photography and get out there and be close to the subjects you love.'

GOLDENEYES ON CHEQUAMEGON BAY, Greg Alexander

"Wow—I had just been granted permission to pursue my dreams on my own terms. I left St. Paul for the south shore of Lake Superior and spent the next four years in a remote log cabin. I figured that the one hundred and fifty-dollar-per-month rent was a pretty cheap tuition for my self-guided education. I wandered endlessly through the forest building up a wealth of reference photographs.

"For more than twenty years, my art has been paying the bills and I have remained dedicated to continuing my pursuit. Dedication is not always glamorous, but the passion it kindles has allowed me to successfully convey the images I see to others. I'd like to think my love for hunting and fishing is what brought out the artist in me and my passion for God's creation has never been more alive in my work."

RETURN OF COASTER BROOKIES, Greg Alexander

14

# Perpetuating the awe of nature

Gary is a self-taught artist who was law school bound when he realized that his true passion was in using watercolor to depict the complexity and awe-inspiring mystery of nature. Gary hikes and canoes in wilderness areas and national parks, searching for the scenes he likes to paint. His work suggests a sense of place that viewers can readily identify with and appreciate.

EAST ROSEBUD CREEK, Gary Spetz

NORTHWOODS FALLS, Gary Spetz

"There have been times when I have found it difficult to complete a painting, but never do I remember lacking the desire to begin one. The drive to paint is a constant force within me. It is fueled, simply, by a reverence for wilderness. My eyes perceive, in nature, elements of color and design, which, for some intangible reason, are pleasing. For most of those fortunate enough to experience this same pleasure— this awe of nature—it is a fleeting feeling. But, for the artist, I believe, this experience can be quite compelling. The artist is driven to perpetuate this feeling.

"When I arise early and hike a mountain trail or paddle along the rocky shoreline of a calm, reflective wilderness lake, I am often overwhelmed by the mystique of the surrounding natural world. In the early hours, there can be much magic in the wilderness air. Although it cannot necessarily be seen, it can certainly be felt—it is more than the sum of what is visual, to be sure. To walk or paddle within the realm of this mystique is to enter both an imposing and enticing new dimension of the senses. This all-encompassing feeling can be strong and its lure great. At times, it can be literally breathtaking, as your mind attempts to comprehend what seems, to its senses, overwhelming. I suppose that like an addictive drug, this element of mysticism draws upon me. But it is, unfortunately, short lived. As the sun rises, the magic diminishes exponentially. If I could have three wishes in life, one would surely be to halt the clock and make the morning last throughout the day! But, as this seems unlikely, I have sought out a substitute that can help me continue this feeling or this natural high, if you will."

"That, of course, is where the paper, paint and brushes come in. Through art, I attempt to perpetuate the awe. It is a tall order, to be sure. To substitute for the multi-dimensional mystique of nature, an artist must interpret with the tools of color, form and design. Certainly, a photograph can capture an image with accuracy, but it cannot capture the awe. Conveying that element requires artistic intervention—something that is well beyond the capacity of the soulless shutter box.

"On a good day, my paintings can take me back to a time and a place in the wilderness. Photos and value sketches prompt my memories, and all merge at the tip of my brush. Mentally, I am there and the walk through the painting process can be as euphoric as the initial walk through the wild. Truly, the journey, itself, can be its own reward. It is easy to understand why painting is considered to be therapeutic to the soul.

"But, of course, the greatest award is granted when your paintings can stir the memories of someone else. Your mission is fulfilled when your painting can transport its viewer to his or her own time and place. In doing so, you, as an artist, perpetuate the awe of nature in others.

"Wilderness is chocked full of inspiration and a lifetime of paintings! To find inspiration, simply go walk in the woods!"

GLACIER CASCADE, Gary Spetz

BRYCE CANYON OVERLOOK, Gary Spetz

GRINNELL LAKE, Gary Spetz

# Painting on location

One of the essential steps in your journey as an artist is to experience the inspiration that comes from painting on location. The most important reason to paint on the scene is to observe and interpret the constantly changing light. You will find that light transforms the ordinary into the extraordinary. Another important reason to leave your studio is to find renewing and nurturing experiences to feed your soul and heighten your awareness of your surroundings. With your *artist's eye*, you are documenting first-hand the raw beauty of a scene and not the translated or second-generation interpretation of a photograph. Being there with your subject will enable you to create your own personal file of material to draw on for the rest of your life. Exploring new vistas on location takes courage. There are distractions, uncooperative weather, changing light, and many other factors that can be challenging, but the experience of being totally involved with your subject is worth the effort.

This scene is typical of the little hill towns found in Umbria, Italy. The light dancing around and creating patterns on the stone walls adds excitement to the final interpretation.

Karlyn Holman

This painting was composed and painted on location in a little mountain village in Bulgaria. Subjects were everywhere, but the charm of our luncheon restaurant drew a number of us to this spot. As we painted, our senses were overwhelmed by the smells of the *gyuvech* wafting by our noses, the hand-woven textures of the tablecloths, and the echoing sounds of an artist hand building these charming tables and chairs. The constantly changing light provided us with a continual challenge to our interpretations of the scene.

Karlyn Holman

Driving your car after you have been out painting on location can be dangerous because suddenly you see your surroundings in a whole new light. Your newfound attention to the beauty and detail all around you can be very distracting. You need a sign—

# Danger, Artist At The Wheel

**Sandy Piano** painted this loose and highly expressive interpretation of a sidewalk scene on location in Portovenere, Italy. Using only a few strokes, she truly captured the spirit and personality of the delightful cafés and bustling crowds.

# Discover old world charm first-hand

This sixteenth century museum village of Arbanassi in Bulgaria provided an endless array of old world charm and natural beauty. I started this painting with a cobalt blue underpainting and next painted the trees as patterns of light and dark. Warm colors were then layered on to finish the painting.

**William Barrett** took this delightful photo showing the determination of this artist to capture the scene from the best vantage point. She wanted to be in the best place for the view, even if it meant being next to the recycling.

# History

Historic photos and historic places provide an unending source of inspiration for the artist. Visit a *living museum* by going on location to paint or photograph. Another option is to check out your attic, the local museum, a yard sale, a thrift shop, or visit an aging relative or friend in your search for photos of historic content. Try to think of an opportunity that might expose you to historic resources.

This painting of Reiten's Boatyard in Bayfield, Wisconsin, was painted on location back in the early eighties. The site was registered as a historic site and was a favorite place for artists to come and paint. Eventually the area was purchased and converted to condominiums. Reviewing photos taken from this area evokes a wealth of memories. As I browse through the photos of these beautiful old wooden fishing boats, I am transported back in time and once again I can feel the breeze off the lake and hear the crying of the gulls as the fishermen unload their daily catch.

These paintings of the same boatyard are part of an eighty-foot mural depicting the history of Bayfield, Wisconsin. The research I undertook prior to painting the mural was as much fun as completing the actual painting.

Karlyn Holman

Karlyn Holman

Karlyn Holman

# Historical perspectives

All the civilizations and cultures of the world have so much to offer to the aspiring artist. Architecture, monuments, gardens, cathedrals and other attractions are living museums suspended in time waiting for you, the artist, to interpret with color. Your paintings are the most memorable part of travel adventures.

The paintings on these two pages were painted on location on the same day in the medieval town of Riquewihr, France, that dates back to 1049 AD. The cobbled streets, half-timbered houses and flower-clad balconies created a picture-perfect composition. The morning remained overcast, so in this "flat light," it was difficult to perceive depth and shadow, so I wet my paper and proceeded with a wet-into-wet underpainting of local color and shapes. When the sun made a brief appearance, I had my camera ready to capture the patterns of light so I could finish the painting at a later time. If you are painting on location and the light never appears, use this as an opportunity to challenge yourself to rely on your intuition, your past experiences, or your mind's eye to invent shadows and values.

I finished this painting in my studio by adding more warm colors and by overlaying cobalt blue to capture the cast shadows.

Karlyn Holman

22

In the afternoon, the sun came out creating well-defined cast shadows. To capture these shadows, I worked on dry paper using cobalt blue and permanent magenta to create a value study of this moment in time. After I completed the underpainting, I freely layered the warm colors over the cool colors. The basic premise of this method is to work in complements. Use cobalt blue in the underpainting for areas where you will later use colors in the orange range and permanent magenta in areas where you eventually will use a range of yellows.

Karlyn Holman

# Art as visual history

Howard Sivertson's deeply personal interpretations of life form a narration based on stories drawn from his personal experiences and his fascination with the history of his area. His paintings provide a rare visual journal of decades of living with nature.

## H. SIVERTSON

Voyageurs trading with Indians on the Granite River, mid 1700's.

Howard Sivertson

"When considering all the directions your art could take, you may want to explore historical painting as a viable option. Many national historic events have been well documented by very famous and competent artists while photographers and artists of the times have relatively ignored local historic events. It's surprising how little we know of the visual history in our own back yards. Before the 1840's and the invention of photography, the only pictures we have were rendered by artists who in many cases did not witness the event, but were hired to recreate it to favor the viewpoint of the person who commissioned the art. Even after photography became common, there wasn't always a photographer or artist on hand to record the event.

"In digging through the history in Northeastern Minnesota, I've found countless stories of historic significance that should be documented visually. Photographers can't take pictures of yesterday. Only interested artists with skill, imagination and patience for research can recreate history visually.

"Twenty-five years ago, when I started painting full time after leaving a career in graphic arts, it was natural for me to paint the dramatic landscapes that surround my studios in Grand Marais, Minnesota, and Pine Bay, Ontario. Since then, I've been wandering at will through the wilderness of the Boundary Waters Canoe Area, the North Shore of Lake Superior, and Isle Royale in search of subjects. Painting landscapes has always been a natural expression of my love for my homeland. After a few years of painting the raw wilderness, I started including subtle suggestions of man's presence. When I stumbled on ruins of an old trapper's shack tucked on the edge of a remote river, I found it interesting to reconstruct the cabin the way it might have looked 100 years ago, along with the trapper's canoe, tools and implements of his trade. I've resurrected many fish houses, old boats and logging camps in the same manner since then."

Muskeegoe Indians leaving Isle Royale for Grand Portage, 1795.

Howard Sivertson

"In the process I became involved in researching these subjects for authenticity and found fascinating ideas for many more paintings. There are countless subjects awaiting discovery in local historical societies, museums and libraries, waiting to be illustrated, to be seen for the first time. Old-timers are another source for colorful stories that fill their memories and could fill your canvases. There are still a few old folks in my area who can relate stories of pioneering escapades that have become fascinating to us over time.

"My curiosity about my area's past increased dramatically one day while I was sketching on a canoe trip in the boundary waters. The scenery still looked the way it did 200 years ago. I imagined how much more interesting my painting would be if I included a voyageur canoe brigade on its way from the far Northwest Territories heading for rendezvous at Grand Portage on Lake Superior. All I had to do was find out what the canoes looked like, how the voyageurs dressed and learn about the details of paddles and fur packs. After a few months of research, I was able to put the pieces of the puzzle together on a full sheet of watercolor paper and, voila, there it was. I finally saw for the first time how the scene may have looked 200 years ago. After several more years of research and many paintings, I published my second book, *The Illustrated Voyageur*.

"My first book, *Once Upon an Isle*, evolved from a series of oil paintings documenting the now extinct commercial fishing culture on Isle Royale where I had grown up and started life as a third generation fisherman in the Sivertson family. Documenting their lives was a labor of love, and without these paintings, the memory of those colorful, industrious people would have faded completely. I find making the past come alive with paintings far more exciting and valuable than all the rest of the art 'isms' put together.

"As one story led to another story, over 160 paintings evolved. Colorful tales along Lake Superior's water trails became paintings of Indians, voyageurs, explorers, priests, lumberjacks, fishermen and pioneers, along with the various early types of watercraft that brought them to the area. Many of these paintings have been compiled into two other books, *Tales of the Old North Shore* and *Schooners, Skiffs and Steamships*. All my books are published by Lake Superior Port Cities, Inc., Duluth, Minnesota.

"If you are a traditional, representational artist with a curiosity about local history, you may find painting historical subjects as fascinating and rewarding as I have. Good luck!"

Howard Sivertson

Jesuit missionary arriving at Ojibway camp on Prince's Bay on North Shore of Lake Superior, 1852.

Howard Sivertson

Steamer Illinois dropping off first settlers at Beaver Bay, North Shore of Lake Superior in 1856.

Howard Sivertson

White pine logging on Pigeon River, 1903.

# Journaling

Many people approach journaling as a method of personal reflection and growth. Keeping a journal may provide you with a means of finding the artist living within you. The actual documentation of your hopes and joys, your fears and anxieties may inspire you to grow as an artist and person. Journaling can become a ritual—a special time you choose to write on a regular basis.

Sara Muender

Ireland entry by Karlyn.

Many artists sketch as well as write in their journals. Think of your journal as a treasure chest of ideas, impressions, reactions and beginnings. Carry it with you and learn to record your thoughts as they occur. Plan your next painting, describe a scene, record a conversation, plan the next five years, dream, or simply draw a rock or a flower. As these entries accumulate, you will build a storehouse of ideas and memories to draw upon for a lifetime.

Sara Muender

# The language of line

the Royal Palace. Stockholm. Sweden. 29 June 1992.
as seen from the rose garden of Skansen...

*Sara Muender*

Sara Muender

Sara loves to improvise and discover. Her eye and her pen line move together to search out her subjects. This way of working adds great character to her very unique style.

"I love to combine humor with a linear format. I document my travels by sketching, rather than photographing the subject. I usually start my drawings at the bottom of the page using a 'blind contour' style of drawing. I place my pen on the paper and start drawing the first thing in my view; it may even be my knees. I go around the shapes and never take the pen off the paper. Even though these drawings are blind contours, I do peek once in awhile. I try to fill up the page and often when I complete a drawing, I will go in and design dark shapes within the contour lines. The most challenging part is not to go too far when filling in the darks."

Sara Muender

"I drew this gentleman while waiting for my dinner at the Astoria Hotel in St. Petersburg, Russia."

Sara Muender

Cafe Figaro
Rethymno Crete
31 May 1994

# Art inspired by your heritage

Mr. Chee is a rare combination of a scholar, a passionate, virtuoso painter and an inspiring, respected teacher. His artistic career has been shaped by his diverse experiences in both Eastern and Western traditions. Mr. Chee has synthesized the ideas and techniques of both traditions and come up with his own innovative style. He has been honored with prestigious awards and his work is represented in numerous collections.

Cheng Khee Chee

Koi 2001 No. 10, Cheng-Khee Chee

KOI 2001 NO. 10. "I have observed and studied Koi since my childhood. I have deep feelings for and a strong attachment to them. Their beautiful color, shapes and graceful movements are very inspiring and irresistible to paint.

"My knowledge of Koi enables me to take an improvisational approach. I did this painting with my saturated wet paper process. The saturated wet paper allows easy lifting, gives soft edges, and maintains a unified background. I soaked the 300# D'Arches cold-pressed paper, painted the negative background and then lifted shapes off the moist surface. I continued to build forms and refine details."

"I was born in China and while in grade school, I learned calligraphy and gained a firm foundation in Chinese brushwork. At age fourteen, I emigrated to Malaysia where I was fortunate to have been introduced to and be influenced by many eminent artists. I was also inspired by watching the Chinese-American artist, Dong Kingman, demonstrate watercolor techniques.

"Malaysia was still a British colony at this time, and English watercolor painting strongly influenced the art community. Since my early training, I have tried to synthesize the concepts and techniques of both Eastern and Western traditions and to combine realism and abstraction to come up with my own innovations. I revere tradition, but I belong to no particular school or style. Studying great Chinese master painters, as well as great American watercolorists, attending workshops and entering national shows have all helped me to find my vision as an artist.

I continue to experiment, explore and constantly search for the most natural way to express my inner feelings. The watercolor medium is closer to Tao than any other medium—the flowing movement of washes, the mystery and nuances, the fact that the artist can let the medium obey its own laws and create wonders in the same way that nature creates her own work. In watercolor painting, the process often times directly influences the content and sometimes determines the content. My paintings are mostly representational and I prefer to begin with abstraction and end with realism.

"I have had dual careers as a librarian and teacher, but I never lost my faith and passion to become an artist. I would like to credit my wife, Sing-Bee, for making it possible for me to fulfill that dream. She has always encouraged me, and with joy in her heart, has shared my vision to be a full-time artist."

FENTING ALLEY, Cheng-Khee Chee

FENTING ALLEY. "I have returned to my birthplace in China every so often. Once I spent some time wandering through the back alleys. I was very much intrigued by the sound, smell, color, shape and movement.

"This painting was painted in my studio based upon some quick sketches and photo references. Although striving for innovation, I feel that the traditional academic approach can better help me capture my experience in this painting."

AUTUMN HIKE, Cheng-Khee Chee

AUTUMN HIKE. "One of the most exciting aspects of Minnesota life is the experience of changing seasons. Colorful thickets of autumn leaves, exciting snow-covered winter trees, exuberant spring blossoms and luxuriant summer foliage have all stirred my feelings and inspired me to paint.

"For this painting, I crinkled Japanese Masa paper, manipulated it to the desired texture, and painted on the wrinkled surface. I feel it is the most natural way to capture the tree forms. The end result is a combination of East and West and abstraction and realism. Realistic images are actually built up from an accretion of small abstract fragments."

CANYON IMPRESSION 2001 No. 1, Cheng-Khee Chee

CANYON IMPRESSION 2001 No. 1. "I was in southern Colorado and Utah a few years back and did a series of paintings titled the *Spirit of Southwest*. In April this year, I visited the Grand Canyon. The awesome, spectacular, magnificent and wondrous view of the canyons and the ever-changing mood of nature strongly inspired my creative passion and started my *Canyon Impression* series.

"For this painting, I used the Chinese improvisational splash color technique but on smooth illustration board treated with glossy acrylic gel medium instead of rice paper. I started the painting with great emotion and concluded it with reasoning."

THE LOST HORIZON NO. 1. "Like anyone else, I have dreams, fantasies, imagination and vision. All of these defy description or expression in realistic works and images.

"I used the ink marbling technique for this painting. I dripped liquid Oriental ink (Sumi ink) gently onto the surface of a pan of clear water, I manipulated the floating ink gently with a finger or stick to form desired patterns and then placed a sheet of dry rice paper over the surface to pick up the ink pattern. I applied color to finish the painting."

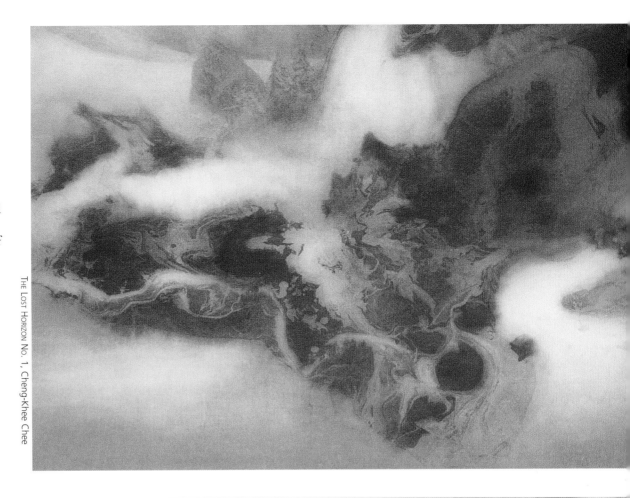

THE LOST HORIZON NO. 1, Cheng-Khee Chee

SPRING TIDE. "An improvisational monoprint image reminded me of my childhood experience of early springtime in southern China: drizzly rain, bountiful water, high tide and sailboats. I developed this image into SPRING TIDE.

"I splashed Chinese ink and watercolor on a piece of white enameled masonite, guided the color and ink to flow and mix in the desired way, and transferred the image to a sheet of absorbent rice paper. After the paper dried, I developed it into a painting."

SPRING TIDE, Cheng-Khee Chee

# Familiar subjects

Celebrate the commonplace. You do not need to go to an exotic destination to find inspiration. The familiar subjects you know and love, the cityscape, your back yard, your family, and still life objects all provide motivation to paint. The same light that transforms nature can create light, shadow and reflection on common subjects you might easily overlook. The most humble aspects of our surroundings are waiting to be explored and elevated. Glance around you. Whether the subject that inspires you is natural or man-made makes no difference. The really important issue is what excites you visually. What is your passion?

Judy Blain

This painting by **Judy Blain** was inspired by everyday subjects and interpreted using a unique perspective. The black and white objects placed on these angular shapes give a somewhat abstract design to the composition.

Karlyn Holman

The photo that served as an inspiration for this painting was taken after an incredible snowstorm that dumped more than twenty-two inches of snow overnight. Although this winter scene is taken from my own back yard, it fit perfectly into a children's picture book illustration for *Ditch of Witches* by Warren Nelson. The witches are merrily flying away after stirring up a blizzard the townspeople "won't soon forget."

**Judy Blain's** clean, direct style transformed these ordinary household objects into inspired paintings.

This painting is one of a series of experiments that Judy painted to see how objects reflect on colored foil papers. It started with Christmas balls on various colors of wrapping paper. Mostly, she was curious to see how a painting of that subject would look. This experimentation led to trying fruit and vegetables on wrinkled or folded papers.

# Urban Slice

Mike takes ordinary subject matter and elevates it to an intriguing composition of color and form. He paints American cities, such as Chicago, Kansas City and Pittsburgh, and focuses on the historical and architectural features of buildings, colorful signs and the energy of the urban setting.

*Mike Welton*

DESCENDING COLOR II, Mike Welton

"Art has always been a nurturing element in my life. Ever since childhood, I have reacted to my environment through artistic means. I would draw something that attracted me, such as a car, and then recreate it, redesign it, or draw it in an imaginary place. I still use that same method to portray what I love in new and insightful ways.

"As a participant in the Art Buddies program, where I mentor, one-on-one, inner city children in producing art, I have gained an additional appreciation for enjoying my creative processes through teaching.

"*Urban Slice* is my series dedicated to capturing the disappearing inner city landscape, where our American individuality is expressed from the late nineteenth to early twentieth century in houses, signage and buildings. Each *Slice* strives to catch a building's historical and environmental presence in directional lighting. I liken it to my personal expression of urban preservation. I observe the architectural design of buildings several ways before deciding on the makeup of visual elements. To capture details or try variations of color schemes, I may paint a couple of different compositions within one. Every piece combines a sensitive, substitutive use of structural features ultimately combined in the composition to become a unified design."

RAINBOW WINDOWS, Mike Welton

"The painting, REMINISCENT, is one painting of many in the *Urban Slice* series influenced directly by the city of Pittsburgh. This city's intriguing close housing quarters on steep landscape with moving shadows of daytime light create a visual impact unlike any other city. The clean classic lines of the homes and the playful bright colors help accentuate the closeness and the angles, resulting in the creation of beautiful designs.

"I formulate my pictures by an immediate response method. I walk the streets looking for a subject matter that may or may not show itself depending on the time of day and the daylight effects. I then study the area and take several pictures from many angles and perspectives. I allow the camera lens to be my picture frame.

"The dynamics of my paintings are manifested through the simple expression of light, shape and color. The subtle to stark contrasts of my palette underline the excitement."

# Seeing with your mind's eye

## MH RICE

All art starts with the dream or the vision within each of us. Mary's paintings are motivated by her mind's eye, an inexhaustible treasure-trove of images, triggered by her memories of childhood tea parties, favorite places, lifelong interests, travels and countless other familiar sources of inspiration. She approaches her painting with little planning and simply lets the image evolve.

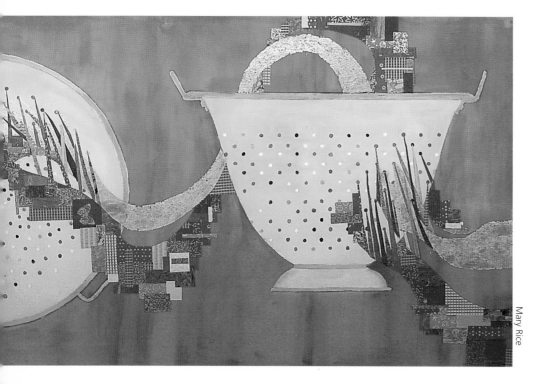

Mary Rice

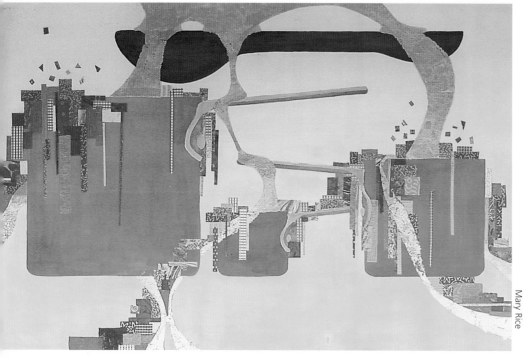

Mary Rice

"For someone who had been searching for her art medium as erratically and as long as I had, it certainly was a great relief to finally discover watercolor and its limitless possibilities. At forty-plus, I finally found the courage to show others my images, and after taking a couple of watercolor lessons, I found my world.

"Finding my own path in this world was closely tied to the medium itself. As I learned to control what needed to be controlled and let flow what needed to flow, I began to feel inspired to continue to push the limits of the water media world. In order to be able to do that, I found it was easiest and more fun to work with familiar images—initially from both photos and still lifes—and then from my imagination.

"The exploration has been a challenge and more fun than I could ever have imagined. Each time I learned a new technique, met a teacher, or hung out with a group of artists, I felt like a huge sponge, absorbing, storing awesome tidbits to be tried, modified, experimented with and all added to the well of inspiration.

"My latest adventure along this path is quite a combination of elements. My first serious art form was food preparation, which I have done for fun and professionally for fifty years. For the opening of my new restaurant, I wanted to hang some of my work, but the paths I had previously explored were either well documented or not appropriate subject matter. In addition, my desire or need to experiment with gold leaf loomed large in my dreams. Flowers in outrageous colors might have worked for the new setting, but I came up with another plan."

"'Foodies' (food fanatics) revere an eggplant or a fine whisk or a functional tool and feel they are beautiful. Historically, itinerant, religious artists have captured certain elements with metals; the Campbell's soup can has become a cultural symbol. In this context, it occurred to me irreverent color, both in paint and collage, gold leaf and the images of the *tools and elements* of my oldest pursuit might be quite a marriage of inspiration. I painted, collaged and leafed the *Icon* series, which ultimately included food elements, tools, equipment and wine.

"For me, inspiration always comes as a result of simple problem-solving mixed with comfortable images, ease with media and a certain amount of risk or new technical skills. We all get into ruts and have periods where nothing works. Those periods used to scare me because I could not come up with a decent painting or collage or anything. Now I use these down times to try a new skill (gold leaf) or technique (powdered pigments or collage) to start my juices flowing. These periods no longer seem anti-productive, but actually become valuable learning times."

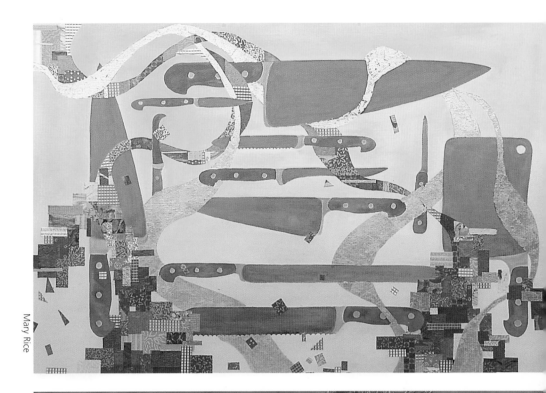

Mary Rice

Mary Rice

"Imagination and images and techniques and tools all conspire for the artist to have 'way too much fun.' Inspiration is always the compendium of all the elements of your life, but springs especially from those subjects you see, feel or think about all the time. Sometimes familiarity does not breed contempt, but instead gives birth to inspiration and success. It is much easier to learn a new technique or try an experience when you are familiar with the size or shape of what you wish to portray. Delving into your memory bank and pulling out images then becomes exciting and leads to inspiration—a way to combine the familiar with a new interpretation. Then it is a quick step to starting down a whole new, totally personal path to an inspired work!"

# Art as a
# spiritual quest

*Jan Hartley*

Jan's paintings convey a truly personal expression that is the result of years of study, meditation and journaling. Jan explores the spirit world through her paintings, which are far removed from direct, visual observations. While her imagery has a feminine base, her message speaks to both genders.

"My inspiration comes from my inner spiritual life. Images surface from my ongoing and deeply personal relationship with the source of life, guiding my spiritual growth and healing and bringing me to a new level of spiritual understanding.

"Access to the spirit world occurs during daydreams, night dreams, meditations and shamanic journeys. By emptying my mind of all thought, I allow room for the new images to emerge. Years of experience and honed technical skills allow me to give visual form to such abstract images.

"The images come to me in series, as parts of a larger whole. The images are intensely personal to my life experiences but seem to have an archetypal spiritual energy that speaks to a larger population. The energy of these images helps me share with others the major themes and similarities in our shared life path."

AXIS MUNDI, Jan Hartley

GROUNDING MOTHER, Jan Hartley

"This image of women as the axis of the world speaks to the reproductive capacity of the human female and the generosity of her nurturing commitment to the future generations. Female ancestors provide the foundation upon which the current generations stand and offer hope to future populations to be strong, gentle, creative and fully authentic."

"This image enables us to stand on the earth, fully grounding us into our human selves, which allows us to open to our spirit selves, and by integrating body and spirit, we fully experience our earth walk. We are spirit made flesh for this journey."

EARTH BORN, Jan Hartley

"This image speaks to our need to be fully human in order to be birthed into the cosmos. Being aware of our animal nature as it is married to our spirit brings us into the wonder of creation."

TRANSFORMATION, Jan Hartley

"We are called many times during our Earth walk to cast off our old way of being in order to allow space for the mystery to bring forth the new. These initiations occur many times during our life. Being aware allows the experience to bring transformation."

# Art as a healing journey

Marsha has created an expression in her work that goes beyond representational art. She has translated her physical trials into a new language of visual imagery.

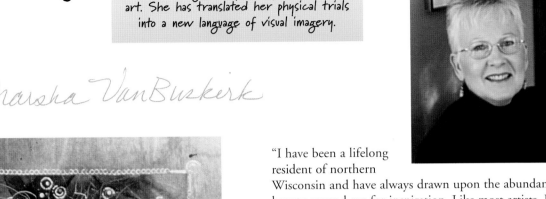

Marsha VanBuskirk

"I have been a lifelong resident of northern Wisconsin and have always drawn upon the abundant beauty around me for inspiration. Like most artists, I find that my paintings evolve with time and experience, with nature most often providing the subject and the *spark*. As I matured, I began to realize that my work failed to fulfill a need I had to express myself in more abstract and symbolic ways. Most of my efforts looked and, more importantly, felt superficial and contrived.

"An extended study trip to China in 1987 became the impetus for the change I desired. When I returned, I started combining traditional Chinese brush techniques and materials with Western concepts and media to create semi-abstract collages. But the most significant changes in my work came a short time later while I was learning to identify and cope with chronic illness. My personal experience with illness, however painful, became my source of inspiration and propelled me even closer to the goal of producing meaningful, abstract works."

REKINDLING THE BRIGHTEST STAR, Marsha Van Buskirk

REKINDLING THE BRIGHTEST STAR. "This severed image of Venus came about at a time when my illness was undiagnosed. I felt as though the physical and intellectual parts of my being were not in sync. The color red is very symbolic of pain."

BEYOND THE RED, Marsha Van Buskirk

BEYOND THE RED. "This piece represents my struggle between pain (red) and well-being (blue). The large circle symbolizes wholeness of body, mind and spirit."

"The following pieces were created using mixed water media on a rice paper support. I began each with a traditional Chinese brush painting technique called 'washed ink.' Chinese ink was allowed to float on the surface of a paper that had been flooded with water. As the water evaporated, residues of ink were left in interesting, random patterns. When the ink was completely dry, the images were developed using various water media. The approximate size of each is 27" by 32"."

"The group of four mixed-media pieces reproduced here represents the most personally satisfying and powerful work I have ever created, and these pieces have become part of the healing process for me. Each one took form in my heart and soul before being brought to my consciousness as a nearly complete image. Not only have I learned the importance of creativity in maintaining good health, I have continued to listen to my spirit and soul when making art."

CELESTIAL NECKLACE, Marsha Van Buskirk

CELESTIAL NECKLACE. "This piece came about when I was finally diagnosed and the pain started to respond to management techniques. Yellow is the color of hope, as is the sun image, and the snake represents metamorphosis or the promise of change."

BREATH OF LIFE, Marsha Van Buskirk

BREATH OF LIFE. "The turtle started appearing unexpectedly in my life and is used in my work as a symbol of life, well-being and Mother Earth. The color blue also symbolizes health and well-being. In this piece, as well as the others, I tried to suggest the ever-present, ever-nurturing elements of the universe— water, earth, stars, moon, etc."

# Inspiration by trial

*John Murphy* [signature]

This very personal series of mixed-media about Elizabeth shows how expressing your emotions can be a healing experience. John Murphy's art was driven by circumstances over which he had no control, and making these images brought some comfort in facing the pain in his heart.

"Inspiration for my art has come from my family, my wife, Lisa, and my daughter, Elizabeth—the ones I love most. With the birth of my daughter, Elizabeth, I found a whole new world of inspiration as I watched her grow. As she discovered the world around her, my art became simpler and I began to concentrate on form, color and structure. When Elizabeth was thirteen months old, she was stricken with Wilm's tumor, a cancerous tumor of the kidney. Our lives changed at that moment—both hers and ours. One of her kidneys was removed and six months of chemotherapy was prescribed. Her illness consumed us twenty-four hours a day. At this time in my life, every human emotion I ever had was magnified ten-fold—love, hate, frustration and sadness. By continuing with my art and expressing my emotions through the photographs of Elizabeth, she, in so many ways helped me to cope with what she was going through and, in turn, I was able to stay focused on the love and support she relied on from me.

"I photographed Elizabeth in black and white and then I cut out the photos and reconstructed them on layers of glass using paint as an accent. I then rephotographed these constructions in color."

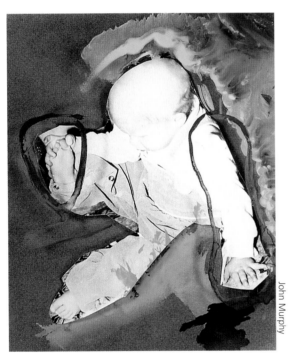

John Murphy

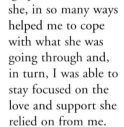

John Murphy

John Murphy

John Murphy

John Murphy

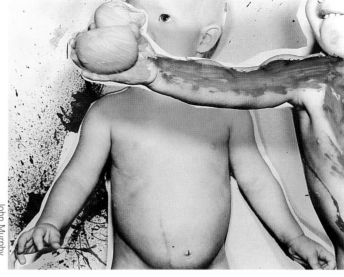

John Murphy

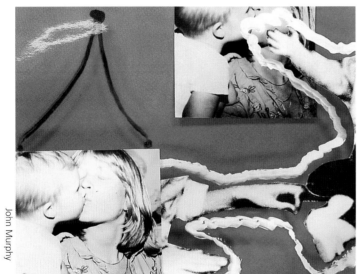

John Murphy

John Murphy

John Murphy

John Murphy

"Elizabeth graduated from high school this year and I decided to finally share this very personal series with her for the first time."

## CHAPTER 2

# Understanding the elements of design—learning the essential skills for self-expression

One of the essential steps along your journey as an artist is to gain an understanding of the universal elements of design and the infinite capabilities of watercolor. These design elements are not restricting or inhibiting, nor are they rules. Your vision will evolve based on your understanding and use of these basic **guidelines** and you will learn to use them intuitively as you paint. Few media can capture your emotions as well as watercolor. One of its greatest attributes is that it lends itself to change and new direction. The tools, techniques and elements of design you eventually choose will fuel your passion.

Sunflowers are one of my favorite subjects because they have almost human-like attributes. Sometimes they appear proud and other times tired or sad. Sunflowers also provide dynamic design possibilities because of their large size and deep colors. This painting started out with a drawing. Next I painted the sunflowers and then masked over the color. By protecting the flowers with masking, I was able to paint a very free wet-into-wet background. The rectangular shape in the background was created with masking tape to form a contrasting hard edge. I continued to draw more sunflowers until I felt the painting was resolved.

# Line

Line is as unique as its creator, as old as civilization and as varied as its function. Line provides movement, perspective and, most importantly, expression. Line is the key ingredient in our visual language. Line is easy and direct and can go beyond an outline or contour into depicting a three-dimensional form. Line may also create light and shadow, mood, texture and energy. Lines can be a work of art in themselves.

Line is the most direct approach to starting a painting. In this portrait of Rachael, the line defined the contour and established the proportions, but most importantly, the line gave me the confidence to interpret value and shape using color.

Karlyn Holman

To complete this drawing/painting, I used my brush like a drawing tool, using only the color indigo. To keep this painting as simple as possible, I painted Rachael as only a positive shape.

46

As you gain more experience and increase the complexity of your subject, the use of line helps to define the relationship of the parts. For example, this montage of Rachael goes beyond outlining the subject because I also added a background. Using black and white photocopies, I searched for the lines to describe the composition. The interplay of positive and negative shapes was pure joy to create.

# Drawing with watercolor

Lines can be expressive of a person's character. This elderly gentleman looked like he stepped out of another century. As he wandered around our painting site in Bulgaria, he was very friendly in a quiet way and allowed us to photograph him. Other characters in the area could not figure out why we did not want to photograph them. They posed for us and became very upset with us when we showed no interest in them as a subject.

Drawing this subject was so much fun, I found it hard to stop drawing and start painting. I did not want to lose any of the energy of the pencil lines, so I finished the work by *drawing* with color.

Karlyn Holman

Karlyn Holman

48

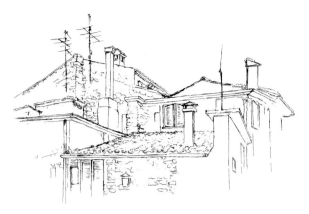

Watercolor is fresh and spontaneous; when you paint, you are actually drawing. Watercolors have been called "liquid drawings." In museums, curators classify watercolors as *works on paper* and usually store and conserve them along with the drawings. Watercolors and drawings are considered finished works of art.

This facade of Umbrian buildings is a treasure of textures and shapes waiting to be interpreted. If your painting does not satisfy your emotional response to the subject, you can continue searching for your personal expression by drawing over the watercolor.

# Drawing

*"A drawing is an invention."*
*Robert Henri*

Drawing is the beginning of your search because drawing gives you a way to express your ideas, capture what you see and portray your feelings. Drawing is also fine art in its own right. Drawing is the starting point of the creative process and one of the most essential steps in finding your artistic identity. A basic knowledge of drawing fundamentals is your ticket to freedom and discovery, allowing you to translate your ideas to the two-dimensional surface.

Drawing is an intuitive and instinctive activity and a skill you can learn, develop and practice. We all knew how to draw as children, but many of us managed to forget this skill when we grew up. For example, artists instinctively created the drawings in prehistoric caves. If you have the desire, these forgotten skills can be developed again. Drawing is not difficult. You simply must make the commitment to learn the principles and

techniques and then practice. The line you make on the paper is coming from your heart and only you can make that line. Drawing is a continual source of inspiration and your ticket to translating your personal thoughts and feelings into a visual form.

No matter how you start a painting, there must be a planning process. Sketching will give you confidence and help you feel centered before you begin. It is like stretching before you exercise. You can stretch your ideas and warm up your painting beforehand. The time spent planning helps give you direction. For some artists, this means lots of drawing prior to the start and no visible drawing on the actual painting. For these artists, drawing serves as a means to start their creative juices flowing. When they actually start their paintings, they start with a blank page and intuitively let the work evolve.

For many artists, drawing provides the foundation for a painting. Improving your drawing skills gives you confidence and helps you find new ways of expression to capture the real spirit of your subject. As your drawing ability improves, you will become more and more selective as your heart guides you to find your personal expression. The pencil and eraser represent freedom, so keep experimenting and changing until you find what your heart wants to express. Once you achieve the drawing you want, you are free to paint your vision.

The most important first steps in your search are to gift yourself with time and to find ways to keep your energy flowing. Give yourself the same gift you would give a child: access to materials, time, a place to work and, most importantly, nonjudgmental approval. Remember, this is not a search with a beginning and an end;

it is a circle of starts, discoveries and explorations. At times, learning formal design elements, understanding techniques, and finding your own expressive style may seem like an impossible goal, but with determination and hard work, you can do it. Celebrate who you are and let your personality shine through your paint.

Rachael's intense blue eyes do not show in this pencil drawing, but her mischievous personality is reflected in her little *Mona Lisa* smile.

I have been privileged to spend a great deal of time in Hope Town in the Bahamas, and this colonnade of palm trees lining an intimate pathway has always inspired me to draw. The sweeping movement and interlocking shapes create a dynamic design.

# Directional movement

Artists need to be aware of how the movement and energy created by the directional placement of shapes help lead the viewer's eye through the artwork. For example, if you use straight horizontal lines, the static composition conveys a sense of serenity or calm. By designing with oblique shapes, you will be able to lead the viewer's eye in specific directions. Keep this in mind as you create passive horizontal lines or dynamic angular lines.

Karlyn Holman

This simple lakeshore painting has strong horizontal shapes breaking up the vertical trees. A grayed painting like this evokes an emotional feeling of serenity, softness and peacefulness. You can almost hear the subtle ripples in the water.

Karlyn Holman

This abstraction has static shapes and limited, analogous colors with a large amount of white space. The overall feeling conveyed by this painting is a feeling of quiet calmness.

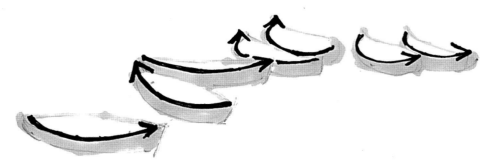

This drawing of boats in the Vernazza harbor has more dynamic angles that shift directions and pull the viewer's eye along from left to right. A strong vertical line of movement is also created by the reflections in the water.

This underpainting establishes a range of values from light to mid-tone by using cobalt blue, permanent magenta and Antwerp blue.

The painted version of BOATS IN VERNAZZA has
a muted, neutralized background, which adds
an unfocused, atmospheric quality. I wanted the
background to be simple and unobtrusive so
the boats could have center stage.

# Shape

Shape is defined as positive, negative or overlapping and can be reduced to simple forms such as circles, ovals, rectangles or squares. Shapes should describe your subject. By varying the edges so some are lost and some are found, you can create visual excitement in your paintings. Shape creates a sense of depth on a two-dimensional surface. One of your biggest challenges when designing a composition is to establish a relationship among the shapes and ultimately connect the shapes into a design. One of your best tools as a shape-maker is designing interlocking and overlapping shapes that include a variety of sizes. Shapes in your composition usually need an entry (foreground), a development (center of interest), and a distance (negative space).

Sara Muender

This drawing by Sara Muender shows how the use of **interlocking** and **overlapping** shapes leads the viewer into her composition.

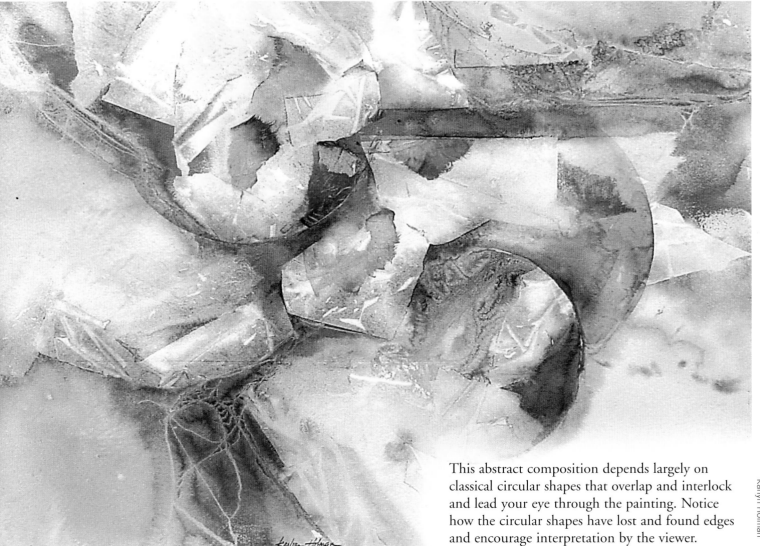

This abstract composition depends largely on classical circular shapes that overlap and interlock and lead your eye through the painting. Notice how the circular shapes have lost and found edges and encourage interpretation by the viewer.

Karlyn Holman

A line of boats in Vernazza, Italy, formed the basis
for a fantastic abstract composition of varying shapes
that interlock and repeat to form a strong design.

# Shapes and values working together in a composition

These fishermen in China were very relaxed considering how many lines they were tending. The interlocking and overlapping shapes create a feeling of perspective.

This drawing shows only the contour lines or outside shapes of the fishermen.

The same drawing can be interpreted in value by using value pens. This quick preliminary step helps give you the confidence to start the larger painting.

This underpainting shows the values developed in a range of cobalt blue and Antwerp blue.

Warm colors were layered over the cool colors to complete the painting.

Karlyn Holman

# Sara Muender

Sara Muender is a true shape-maker. Her strong compositions, combined with her unique color sense, have produced a signature style of work. Sara combines watercolor with linear shapes to create an inspiring diversion from soft, transparent watercolor. These mixed-media paintings are structured with simple shapes outlined by pens.

BABY TANG, Sara Muender

MANATEE, MANITOO...MANA-ME, MANA-YOU, Sara Muender

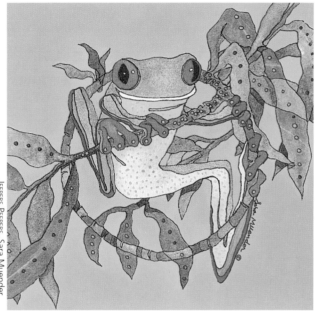

JEEPERS PEEPERS, Sara Muender

These graphic designs by Sara Muender are an excellent example of how shapes and complementary colors work together to make a strong statement.

BODACIOUS BLOSSOMS, Sara Muender

# *Letting your spirit lead you*

*Karen Knutson*

"I remember when I first noticed that I was ready to make *the change* in the direction of my artwork. I'd been painting for approximately fourteen years and had interpreted a wide variety of subjects including flowers, landscapes and illusionary and abstract ideas. One day, I realized how disappointed I was when my clients were more interested in my landscapes than my recent abstract paintings. Soon after, I was on a painting trip in Italy and we had been painting archways and buildings for about two weeks. One day, I decided to throw perspective out the window and paint a doorway in an abstract manner. I had found my new direction!

"For many years, my abstracts were totally nonrepresentational. Now, I love combining realism with abstraction. The paintings shown here are from my recent series, *Musical Women.* One of the biggest hurdles that I have had to overcome is **simplifying** shapes. I have learned to really think about values and shapes and to inspect my painting afterwards and make sure that there is a **focal area** using only **one** of the values. I still enjoy painting landscapes occasionally to remind myself of the beauty of the North Shore along Lake Superior, but my heart and soul will always be in painting semi-abstract paintings with lots of color and good design.

MUSIC CONNECTS US ALL, Karen Knutson

MELODY OF THE HEART, Karen Knutson

"Painting in a series is a great way to improve your work. My first series happened quite accidentally. My grandfather from Montana had a real talent for playing piano by ear and often played for local dances. Unfortunately, the talent didn't get passed down through the generations, but my love of music has expressed itself in my paintings and I feel closer to my grandfather as a result of my first series. In the first painting, MUSIC CONNECTS US ALL, my most important goal was to simplify my values into big shapes and connect them. Since I have a tendency to make tiny shapes when I paint, I allow myself to do this in the early stages

of the painting, but then toward the end, I glaze over big areas to connect the shapes and simplify values.

"When I start a painting, I wet most of the surface and float the colors on the paper, letting them mix by tipping the paper and letting drips *happen*. Then I turn it all four directions and try to *see* any images and let the painting tell me which direction to go. The second painting, MELODY OF THE HEART, turned into a cello player when I saw all the drips that resembled guitar or cello strings."

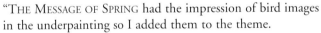

Message of Spring, Karen Knutson

The Cat's Meow, Karen Knutson

"THE MESSAGE OF SPRING had the impression of bird images in the underpainting so I added them to the theme.

"THE CAT'S MEOW was a lot of fun to paint. I hid piano keys on the bookshelves and created the illusion of a cat in the corner. I like to surprise my viewers when they study my paintings, giving them more information than they initially see. This painting received many glazes to increase values and connect the tiny shapes. I often turn paintings upside down to check for balance and to see shapes instead of things. Sometimes I look at my paintings using peripheral vision from about six feet away, thus allowing me to see values much more easily.

"I love painting abstracts because the spirit of my soul comes out and I truly paint from my heart. I try to paint the subject as I perceive it, rather than trying to achieve a realistic interpretation. My latest painting, AFTER HOURS, was truly a pleasure to paint. After allowing the first application of paint to float on the surface, I inspected the painting to see if I could *see* any impressions to suggest my direction. The lady at the bar, pink hair and all, was there as plain as day. All I had to do was add a glass of wine and the other people in the painting. Perhaps this painting will lead to a brand new series."

After Hours, Karen Knutson

# Value

*"Think of values as giving form, not as spots of light and dark."*

*Robert Henri*

Value is the relative lightness or darkness in your painting. Achieving the correct value in watercolor is more difficult than in other media because the value you paint wet is not the value that remains when your paint dries. **The actual value dries about two shades lighter.** Keep this in mind as you plan a range of values in your painting. Values help you see the shapes, establish relationships for overlapping and interlocking shapes, and, ultimately, help you establish an interest area. Light and dark values can create dramatic effects, such as the illusion of a three-dimensional form. Each color has a value. Not all light colors, such as yellow, are light, nor are all blues dark. Check out values by relating them to other colors in your composition.

Think of your subject in terms of three simple values: light, mid-tone and dark. A quick value study will give you confidence and guidelines as to where to place your brushstrokes and will help you create fresh, spontaneous, fun and free interpretations of your subject. This sketch was done using 40% and 60% value pens. These pens reduce subjects to patterns that can be translated into color and value. This value sketch was helpful in creating the simplified shapes in my sunflowers.

These steps show the initial wet-into-wet wash of colors used to capture the soft tones and the abstract movement in the painting. All the edges are soft and the background has the suggestion of out-of-focus shapes. As the wet paint flows and mingles together, the colors begin to soak into the paper. As the paint begins to dry, you will have more control over the edges. By using a "thirsty" flat brush that has had the excess moisture removed, you can lift color to reveal the light of the paper. The petals on the sunflowers were lifted to a light value before the paint was allowed to dry.

Value study.

To complete the painting, more darks were added in selected areas. The energy of the underpainting can be easily lost if you carry your darks too far. Try to add only enough darks to *say* sunflowers without overstating the message.

# Values are relative and depend on the relationship of the values around them

The transposition of light values against dark values and dark values against light values is a relatively simple design exercise as illustrated by this drawing and painting. As artists, we need to be aware of the importance of transposing values. You can control value relationships by arbitrarily making values light against dark backgrounds and dark against light backgrounds.

Karlyn Holman

64

This dynamic painting of watermelons by **Frank Zeller** shows how important a light source is to produce a full range of values and give the illusion of three dimensions. The cast shadows and the dark background add to the visual impact.

Frank Zeller

Billy, Karlyn Holman

My friend, Billy, is a hard-living character who loves to challenge your opinion about controversial subjects. His unique personality and the dark shadows were the inspiration for this work.

# The value of value

*Judy Blain*

Judy Blain is a master of value, color and compositional design. The elegant simplicity with which she directly applies her colors immediately speaks to the viewer. Her subjects are recognizable, but her real strength is the strong abstract design expressed in every stroke. Judy's colorful watercolors are a spectacular feast for the eyes.

"I stopped teaching workshops a few years ago because what I wanted to paint was not something I could teach. I had reached a stage where I needed to set aside or even ignore those principles which I had loudly and frequently insisted on impressing upon my students. To the painters who have mastered the techniques of the medium, I would say this: revisit subjects you have enjoyed painting and do a series of paintings of the same subjects stressing concept over subject. Push yourself to the edge of your comfort level. Be brave."

TOUCAN TRIO, Judy Blain

TREE OF LIFE, Judy Blain

"I prefer to work with my easel in an upright position and directly add 'color on color' to create lush, vivid interpretations of tropical subjects. I am energized by my vivid imagination, as well as my love for plants and animals. I am primarily interested in trying to control where the viewer's eye enters the painting and how it subsequently moves through the composition. I prefer to use dark values to achieve this feat, but I may also employ whites and colors. Sometimes, I can even vary how quickly or slowly the viewer's eyes move through the painting. In most cases, I do have a center of interest, but certainly not always. In fact, over time, creating a specific center of interest has become less and less important to me."

TWO IN A TREE, Judy Blain

TOUCAN CONVERSATION, Judy Blain

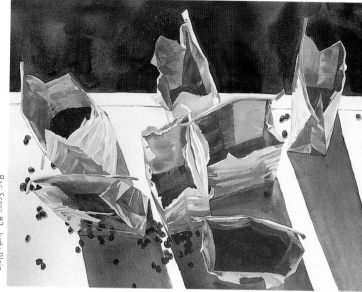

"These *Bag Series* compositions were done from several points of view and helped me become so familiar with the subject that I was freed of the details and the worries about perspective and was able to explore the endless possibilities. After enjoying several interpretations of this image, I added other objects, took the coffee beans out and put flowers in the bags, took the bags indoors, put a mirror behind them and allowed my orange tabby to insinuate himself into the painting."

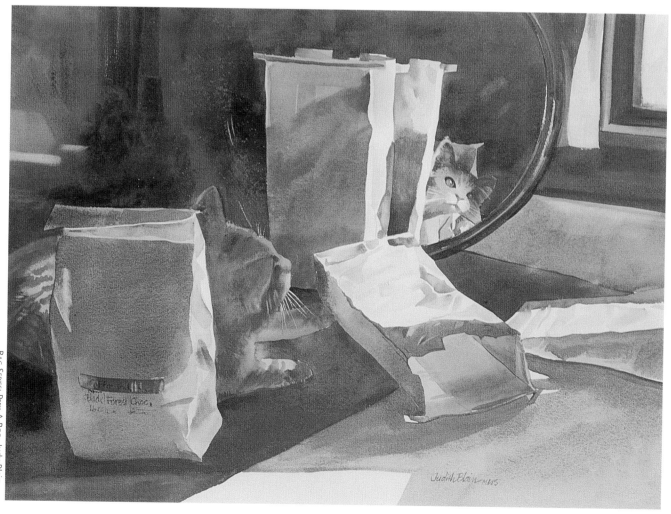

# Color

Color is the most expressive element of art and can move a painting from a mere depiction of fact to one that expresses emotions. Once you learn the basics of color theory, you are free to use your own judgment and intuition when selecting color and intensity. Some colors come forward while others appear to recede. Watercolor can be painted in thin transparent washes or painted so thickly that you can barely see the white paper through the paint. The more color you use, the more energy you transmit to your painting. Transparent watercolor gives us brilliant, luminous color because the light reflects off the white paper.

To understand the **capabilities of color**, you need to understand the inherent properties of the various colors you choose to use. Colors may be staining or non-staining, transparent or opaque, or even whitened or darkened. Take the time to understand each color's personality—it will be time well spent.

The composition of each color is different. Some are made out of clay, some are dye-based, some are mineral-based, and each color's personality will emerge as the color is floating in water on the surface of the paper. Some colors will remain smooth, others will granulate, some will blend and some will separate.

# Color as an expressive tool

The use of **harmonic or complementary colors** allows you to accurately express almost anything you desire. Think of yourself as the conductor of an orchestra. With your paintbrush, you may blend colors, intensify colors, subdue colors or vibrate colors. The choices are endless. As you work more with color, you will choose the colors that fit your personal vision.

Still lifes provide a perfect opportunity to learn about the tools of harmonic and complementary colors because they offer an endless variety of forms, colors and textures. Choose everyday objects or objects with which you have a special emotional connection. Arrange the objects to form overlapping and linking shapes. Each object has a local color and a harmonic or analogous color interpretation, and every shadow has complementary color neutralizing into grays. Be aware of the importance of capturing the light in your still life. Start your still life by drawing directly on the paper with an HB pencil. Erase if necessary with a soft eraser to avoid abrading the paper.

**Harmonic or analogous colors**. By selecting hues next to each other on the color wheel, you can add harmonic depth to your painting. These colors are so closely related that the colors actually flow into each other.

**Complementary colors**. Complementary colors are opposite each other on the color wheel and are an extremely valuable tool for use in your artwork. When complements are used next to each other, they appear more intense and can actually vibrate. The impressionists used this design element in their remarkable paintings. When complements are mixed together, the color will be lowered in intensity until the color is totally grayed. These objects were painted using harmonic color and the shadows were painted using complementary color. For example, the yellow-green grapes have a permanent magenta and orange shadow that was charged with the color of the grape just before the shadow color dried. The tomato shadow started out green and then was charged with red, the lemon shadow started with blue and was charged with orange, etc. There are infinite ways to mix darks. The most obvious way is to purchase the dark pigment, but in order to really create luminous, vital darks, you will achieve better results if you charge complementary colors together on the paper. Using pre-mixed colors or pre-mixing them on your palette can create a flat, dull mixture. Every stroke is the same. By selecting complements from inherently dark values, you can make your own darks.

# The emotional impact of color

An important element in evoking emotion and conveying a particular mood is each artist's choice and use of color. Although a specific subject is usually the basis for each composition, the overall mood evoked by a painting depends most often on the use of color and the dominance of either cool or warm tones.

These two paintings vary in subject matter, but use the same color families. The mood evoked in each painting is largely the result of the warm or cool color dominance.

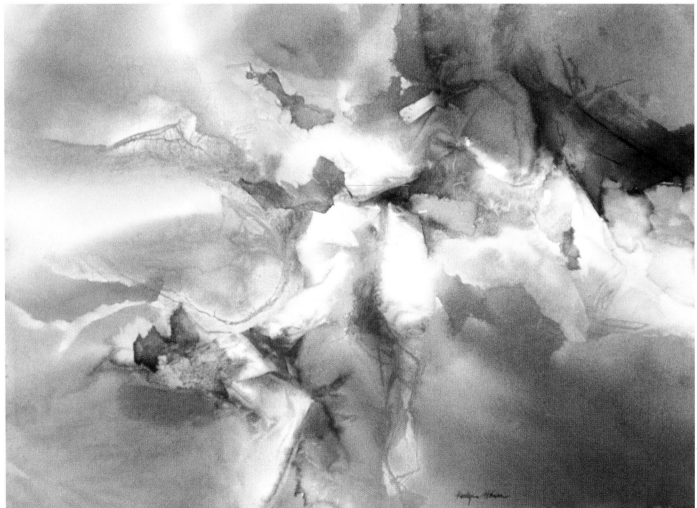

DON'T MESS WITH ME, Sara Muender

These whimsical, crisp designs by **Sara Muender** graphically illustrate how powerful color can be when used to interpret a subject. Sara is a commercial artist with the goal of reaching a specialized market. She is attracted to complementary color combinations with stark, bright colors and high contrast. To help create the mood you want to portray, think about the varying intensities, the range of values and the crisp or soft edges when selecting your colors. Illustrators of children's picture books often use color to visually tell a story. Dark, cool colors create suspense, and warm, vibrant colors depict joy and security.

ANGEL BABY, Sara Muender

JOSEPH'S GOAT, Sara Muender

HOT STUFF!, Sara Muender

MACAW MADNESS, Sara Muender

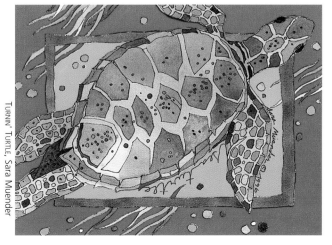

TURNIN' TURTLE, Sara Muender

# Adventures with color

When you view a Rose Edin painting, you are experiencing a visual feast of lively, vibrant color. Rose is a colorist with a unique sense of adventure that has become her signature.

Rose Edin —

THE CAPE OF GOOD HOPE. "This composition was inspired by two photos taken during a trip to South Africa. Some masking was used to save whites and gauze was used on the lobster crates to create textures."

THE TALKERS AND THE THINKER. "This painting was composed from three photographs taken while on an adventure trip to Nepal, India. The first layer of paint was executed using blue values and the warm colors were layered on later."

"I often start my paintings with a wet-into-wet underpainting of primary colors and create textures that set the stage for dramatically keyed values and richly pigmented paint layers. This method of underpainting lends color unity to the composition as the colors flow and meld together, as illustrated in ORGAN MUSIC and WILD ROSES. I layer color over color to achieve a glowing transparent luminosity. I also strive for an energetic contrast of values."

ORGAN MUSIC. "This painting was inspired by a visit to St. Stephens Church in Vienna, Austria. Organ music was playing as the sun was creating patterns of light on the altar. The two figures completed this perfect composition. Some masking was applied to save the whites."

WILD ROSES. "A stand of birches is in full view from my deck, so I painted this scene on location. I picked the roses and placed them in a vase so I could use their color and shapes to create the foreground in the painting."

ORGAN MUSIC, Rose Edin

WILD ROSES, Rose Edin

# Texture

Texture is the surface quality and can be used to stimulate the viewer's tactile sense. A really good translation of surface realism can make the viewer actually want to touch the painting. Surfaces such as old wood, feathers or even lace tablecloths can evoke this tactile sense. This particular design element needs some discretion so as not to be overdone. Techniques for creating texture can be found in the chapter on mastering techniques.

Look for interesting textures in your subjects. These weathered Umbrian doors illustrate the beauty found in everyday objects, and at the same time, they evoke nostalgia for times past.

After you have drawn your subject, paint in the cast shadows and develop a value study using cool tones, such as cobalt and Antwerp blue. While the cool color is wet, you may choose to add a complementary color to create gray tones in the underwash. Texture may be created by adding popcorn salt while the paint is damp.

Layer warm colors over the blue values. Each variation of a warm color will neutralize and gray down the underpainting. In this painting, raw sienna, quinacridone burnt orange and brown madder were layered over the blues. Ultramarine turquoise was used to simulate the remnants of chipped paint from centuries ago.

The final step consists of layering on the darkest values needed to produce the darks. The darks in this painting are brown madder mixed with Antwerp blue. Color was applied using a dry brush technique. Dry brush is accomplished by pulling a paintbrush saturated with paint and a small amount of water over the surface. This dry brush effect is perfect for creating the illusion of textured wood. Finishing details were accomplished by using sandpaper to lift off some color, a razor to carve out some crisp whites and a small brush and painting knife to create the very sharp darks.

# Creating textures with Oriental paper

Collage can be used to add exciting surface interpretation to a traditional subject. You can create a unique textural surface in any of your paintings by gluing down a variety of Oriental papers onto the watercolor paper before you start to paint. Choose white and off-white archival papers and glue them down with YES! paste. It is important to use YES! paste because you will still have a paintable ground in case some of the glue gets on the paper surface.

There is a special energy and challenge generated by working on location. At this site of early Roman ruins in Carsulae, Italy, the sense of history was overwhelming. As I sat with several colleagues and quietly painted this subject, I wondered about all the people who had inhabited this ancient place. The path depicted in the painting is the original Via Flammenia to Rome that dates to the time before Christ. You can still see the chariot ruts carved in these ancient stones.

I usually use a sepia colored, permanent ink pen for my drawings because the softer tone enhances the watercolor. This underpainting was done using cobalt blue and permanent magenta to capture the cast shadows. The foliage was interlaced throughout the ruins to add textural variety.

Karlyn Holman

Next, warm colors were layered over the underpainting to define the color in the stone. The ultramarine blue used for the dark sky added a sense of completion to the painting.

The original entrance into the city of Plovdif, Bulgaria, dates back to the thirteenth century. The eclectic arrangement of the many additions built throughout the following centuries resulted in a unique collection of shapes. The use of several layers of Oriental paper produced exciting variations on the surface of the ground. As each successive layer of color was applied, more and more interesting textures appeared.

Karlyn Holman

You may find these randomly placed papers distracting, making it difficult for you to begin painting. Once again, call upon your sense of adventure and give it a try. This narrow street in an Umbrian village offered many opportunities for interpreting texture. As I painted, children, women laden with shopping bags, construction workers with wheelbarrows, and a myriad of other distractions added to the challenge. I felt like I was in a living collage.

Karlyn Holman

# Concept and composition

Your concept is the most critical part of developing your own style. Any subject can be interpreted into art. Your inner vision will emerge from your own life experiences. You must trust your own intuition and keep searching for your personal vision.

Your composition incorporates all your drawing skills and all the elements of art together to form your concept. The same compositional guidelines apply to both realistic and abstract subjects, but, in general, good composition always starts with good abstract design. Looking for the big picture of abstract shapes before beginning a painting will add strength to your composition.

If you are frustrated by how-to books, consider this a good sign because it means that you are ready to subconsciously connect with a subject and express your emotions in your paintings.

## Finding the driving force for your composition—start with your passion

It is often difficult to know where to start your composition. Should you block in the entire piece, do a thumbnail sketch, or make several drawings to choose from? All of these options are choices to consider. Sometimes it is wise to be driven by the subject itself. If one element of the subject before you is the motivating force that attracts you to paint, then begin with that element. **Start with your passion** and let the rest of the painting evolve.

The drawing of the figure was the driving force in this painting. I purposely placed her near the center and interlocked her shape with the entry door and the shapes in the steps.

My first objective was to capture on dry paper the ever-changing light in a moment of time by using the cool colors of cobalt blue and permanent magenta.

To complete the painting, warm, harmonic colors of raw sienna, quinacridone burnt orange, alizarin crimson, quinacridone gold, Winsor red and scarlet lake were layered on top of the cool colors.

You can evaluate your painting by checking the following universal guidelines:

Try to make one dominant area more entertaining than another and avoid placing it in the exact center in order to break up the remaining areas asymmetrically. Not all paintings have a distinct center of interest, but as a rule, using a variety of dominant and less dominant areas produces a more interesting painting.

Keeping the darkest darks, lightest lights and most in-focus areas close to the center of interest will strengthen your focal area.

Strive for a variety of colors, sizes and shapes.

Connect your painting to the edges so your viewer can enter and exit your painting.

Adding detail, such as figures and textures, adds interest to this dominant area.

Karlyn Holman

Use lines of movement to lead the viewer into the painting.

# Abstract and realistic paintings based on design

John Salminen is a master technician with a unique vision. He paints everyday subjects with artistic virtuosity. His subjects are realistic, but his concepts have strong abstract design.

JOHN T. SALMINEN    AWS DF NWS

"Every time I start a new painting, I face the same intimidating and humbling challenge. I stare at that beautiful blank sheet of pure white paper and think 'what now?' As soon as I make a mark on the pristine surface, I have committed myself to an irreversible process, the end result of which could end up in the fireplace or, ideally, be transformed into an inspired piece of work. Every artist deals with this challenge and every artist approaches it from a different direction, shaped by his/her personal definition of what constitutes a successful painting. My own definition is quite simple—the painting must be an arresting and cohesive design. It is this constant striving to create a strong design that keeps me painting."

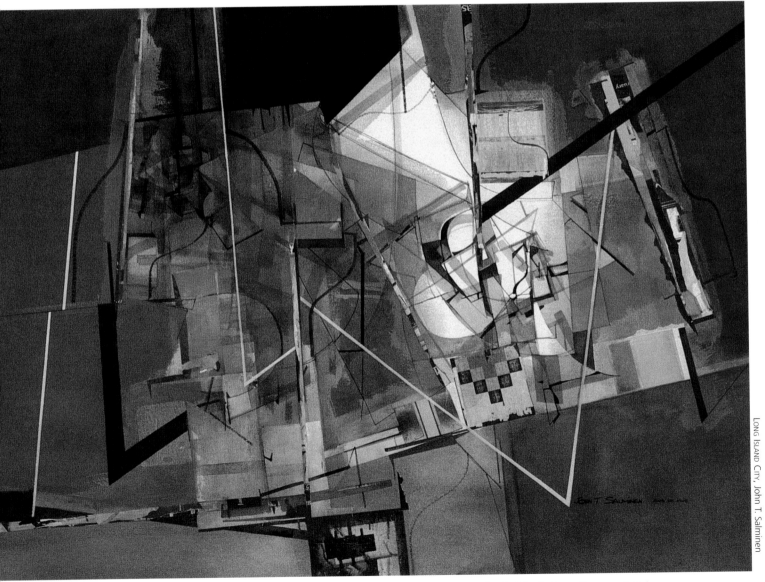

LONG ISLAND CITY, John T. Salminen

LONG ISLAND CITY. "In this abstraction, the design was determined by the placement of the collage materials. My objective was to choose collage materials that were similar in appearance to my painted effects, thereby integrating them into the finished piece. Because I did not want the collage elements to jump out, I avoided recognizable images and looked instead for colors and textures."

86

"I alternate between realism and abstraction in my paintings. While the resulting works look very different, the process and goals are the same. Although I try to work intuitively and spontaneously, I have been so aware of the rules and principles of design that my intuitive decisions are all filtered through my design sensibilities. I stop working frequently to put the partially completed work in a mat under Plexiglas™ and I take a long critical look. If the painting has a problem, I can often solve it by going over my mental design checklist, which is based primarily on Edgar Whitney's approach to design. Once the problem is identified—the shapes lack variety, the forms are not properly linked, the composition lacks balance, etc.— there is usually a design-based remedy. By working instinctively, yet critically analyzing the design, I often find I have created delightful surprises and I am able to avoid sterile formula-based paintings.

"My purest designs are often my mixed medium abstractions because I am not restricted by recognizable images. By adding collage materials, I feel I can overcome my own design clichés. While the resulting paintings are non-representational, I often stage the compositions with the same considerations that I apply to my realistic works. I use atmospheric lighting effects to create a strong center of interest. The reverse is also true—in my realistic work, I am always aware of the abstract nature of the design. If I squint at a completed realistic piece, I hope to see a solidly designed abstraction lurking beneath the surface.

"I am drawn to urban street scenes because of the complexity of the subject. I find unlimited design choices in the overwhelming amount of detail—should I include this, should I play that down, where is my center of interest and how should I stage it? With a busy and often visually chaotic subject, the challenge is to create order out of the chaos.

"Abstraction and realism are the two finished forms my work takes but, from my perspective, the similarities far outweigh the differences. The common unifying factor is **design**."

ROYAL LOANS. "ROYAL LOANS is a Chicago street scene that relies heavily on atmospheric perspective. By allowing the distant buildings to fade and concentrating the lightest values in the background, I am able to draw the viewer's eye through the foreground without becoming lost in the details of the complex storefronts. Without the use of organizational technique, the painting could become visually cluttered."

SECOND MESA. "In this painting, I enlarged a small mixed-medium painting (watercolor, collage and acrylic) and completed it using only transparent watercolor. It was a technical challenge to duplicate the illusion of opacity and collage material. Many of the effects I employ in my realistic paintings worked well in staging the value structure of this piece."

UNTITLED. "This abstract mixed-media painting consists of transparent watercolor, acrylic paint and collage material. I attempt to fully integrate the collage elements so they visually merge with the painted areas. I avoid recognizable subjects when selecting my collage material and look for colors, values and textures that enhance the overall concept."

79 MOTT STREET. "The composition of 79 MOTT STREET could easily have become the basis for an abstraction. The strong dark and light patterns provide the compositional unity while the closely related values provide a rich surface treatment.

It was important to allow some restful areas within the painting, and by working with close values, I was able to downplay certain parts of the design and still show detail and structure."

BRIGHTON VARIETY. "The Brighton Variety store is located in the Russian section of Brooklyn, often called Little Odessa. I was drawn to the light quality of the building facades and the dramatic framing provided by the overhead, elevated train platform."

CHINATOWN MARKET. "In CHINATOWN MARKET, the focus is color. The neutral colors surrounding the fruit stand enhance the effect of the bright oranges and yellow. The cooler parts of the painting consist of grays made from the complements of blue and orange. The figures are not the primary center of interest. I was most interested in the play of light across the colorful fruit."

## CHAPTER THREE

# Mastering techniques—
## choosing the tools that are right for you

*"Fine art is that which the hand, the head, and the heart of man go together."*

*The Two Paths, 1859*

To find your own artistic identity, think of yourself as a craftsperson learning the tools of your trade. The techniques described in this chapter are designed to be **tools** you can use to build your artistic skills and your understanding of the media. Each technique is presented separately, but you will soon see how combinations of these techniques are often necessary to produce a painting. By breaking down and analyzing the techniques one by one, you will begin to see which techniques work best for you.

Knowledge of all the technical expertise available is still not your ultimate goal but, rather, a starting point. Once you learn these techniques, you must put yourself—your soul—into your paintings. The more you work, the more confidence you will gain. When you enter competitions, the two major criteria you will be judged on are your mastery of techniques and the uniqueness of your vision. Give yourself permission to go into this *search mode* and explore for yourself, through trial and error, the path to your own personal style.

Push yourself to work, even on days when you do not feel inspired. After a period of time observing and experimenting, you should begin to see some results. There are many rules and do's and don'ts out there to learn. Make them part of the search, but do not be dominated by them. Art is an expression of your own vision and eventually you will make up your own rules.

# Wet-into-wet

Painting wet-into-wet is the most creative, sensuous and energetic of all the techniques, but, at the same time, it the riskiest method because so much of the action is out of your control. This technique might work one time and not the next. Wet-into-wet is a process of discovery because the paint moves in the water in unpredictable ways. The colors are so sensuous as they meet and mingle and finally blend together. By using a very white paper, you can actually create a glowing effect and build in a luminosity that cannot be achieved any other way.

One of the biggest decisions when approaching watercolor is whether to work wet-into-wet or on dry paper. Each technique produces a finished image with a very distinct personality. You can challenge yourself to be spontaneous by working in wet-into-wet. The movement of the paint in the water forces you to take action and the result is a free-flowing effect. Trust your instincts and let yourself react with the wet paint.

Choose a paper that will not allow the colors to reactivate with each successive layer. I prefer to use Arches cold press. Wet the paper on both sides so the paper will remain flat and stay wet longer. When you wet the paper for the first time, the sizing is activated. Do not soak the paper as this floats away the sizing. When the wet paint meets the wet paper, it is usually love at first sight. As the paint moves with the sizing, you can add more color, move it around by tipping and turning, and even lift the color. The sizing keeps the paint from soaking into the paper so lifting is easier to accomplish. You do not want any interruptions or distractions at this time so you can fully enjoy this magical process. Although you can layer the paint later, you can never experience the same intermingling of colors that happens when the paint is wet. I keep a fine mister handy and continually mist the surface to extend the working time. Use gentle, sweeping strokes to evenly mist the area. In your first wash, do not worry about the realism of your images. Now is the time to create simple, abstract shapes.

Save whites and work as long as you can until you reach the dangerous time when the paper has started to dry in some places. When you reach this stage, it is better to let the paper completely dry because uneven drying may result in "bleed-backs."

The next step is more difficult because you do not want to lose the free-flowing abstract quality you have created, yet you want to add the darks and more intense colors needed to complete the painting. For most paintings, this means adding crisp color and shapes on the dry paper. Be sure to incorporate subtle changes of harmonic color to add depth to your finished painting.

# The first wash—a mixture of pure color and water

This scene in Vernazza, Italy, has all the symbols and shapes an artist lusts after—umbrellas, laundry, people, shutters, peeling paint and foliage. With all these unique details to capture, I had as much fun penciling the drawing as I did applying the first wash. If you like a loose, free-flowing look to your paintings, then a wet-into-wet first wash is a great way to interpret almost any subject. This wet-into-wet underpainting was a study in harmonic and complementary color theory applied as pure color over pure color. The orange building was created by applying the harmonic colors of yellow first and red later. The purplish stone was created by applying the complementary colors of raw sienna and permanent magenta. The greens were created by first "throwing" yellow paint onto the paper and next throwing blue paint into the yellow puddles. All the colors were allowed to mix on the wet paper.

The dark values and crisp detail were completed on dry paper.

# Lifting

Watercolor has special concerns because in order to retain the white of the paper and the transparency of the colors, you must understand techniques that will help save these lights. Lifting is a very basic, yet critical, technique used to save whites and to help you achieve a fresh look in your paintings. Lifting can be done at many stages in the process of painting. The first lifting usually occurs during the wet-into-wet process. While color is floating on the sizing, the color will easily lift to reveal the whites or lights of the paper. Lift with a thirsty brush, tissue, sponge or any absorbent tool.

Lake Superior's fury was captured by lifting color with a brush, tissue and later with a razor blade. Some of the texture was achieved by using salt.

This interpretation of northern lights was created by wetting the paper and applying wet-into-wet warm, harmonic colors on the surface and allowing them to dry. Next, cool, dark colors were layered over the warm colors. Before the cooler color dried,

I used a tissue to lift away color to reveal the warm colors of the underpainting. The important key to this lifting process is to lift away the color before it dries. Once the color soaks into the paper, you can never achieve this same luminous effect.

# Lifting on dry paper

You can also lift the color from a dry painting. The techniques used for this method of lifting usually entail a little more effort. A stiff brush, sandpaper, Q-tips®, sponge, toothbrush, razor, plastic stencil, eraser or even running water may be used.

Karlyn Holman

This subject was painted over the course of a full day on location in Vernazza, Italy. This painting had many layers of paint built up on the surface, and after the painting dried, I decided to lift out dramatic light effects. I placed the painting under running water and scrubbed away the layers of paint with a soft toothbrush, thereby creating the white accents of the light filtering through the buildings and bouncing off the umbrellas. You can accomplish this same effect by immersing the painting in water and scrubbing it with a stiff brush. This sounds like a desperate act, but this technique adds visual excitement you could not accomplish any other way. Let the water in watercolor come to your rescue and not only save a painting, but take it into another realm. A ghost of the undercolor will remain as the lifted whites emerge. This ethereal, soft texture can add an almost spiritual quality to any painting.

# Lifting to create atmospheric perspective

Painting landscapes provides many opportunities for lifting color. The changing light of the four seasons, the constantly moving patterns of white in water, and the unpredictable light in a snow scene are all examples of patterns that you can simulate by lifting the color to reveal the white of the paper.

When beginning a landscape, set the stage by applying wet-into-wet moody color washes. Then create luminosity in the colors by lifting the paint using one of the following techniques.

Karlyn Holman

You may take away some of the color by spraying it away with a coarse sprayer. A soft tissue may be used to lift away colors and create the look of clouds or the mist rising up from the water. A thirsty brush is the perfect tool for capturing the whites in the water. After the paint begins to dry, you can add a little salt to absorb the color and create little white shapes. A scraper may be used to reveal small textures, such as grasses or rocks.

To achieve the impression of light coming through the trees, scrub away the color with a sponge or damp tissue, creating a mysterious look.

# Lifting to create an atmospheric feeling

The atmospheric tempering we see in nature is easily accomplished by using complementary colors and allowing them to mix on the paper. As the colors neutralize, they become grayer and grayer. When you lift away this neutralized color with a soft tissue, the atmospheric quality of the painting is enhanced. As you lift blended colors, there is almost always an element of surprise. Non-staining colors may lift, staining colors may remain, some colors may intensify and others may fade.

A preliminary sketch will help you to visualize your finished painting. You will find this preplanning is tremendously helpful when you are developing an interpretive watercolor. Although your sketch is a blueprint for the work, the actual painting will take on a life of its own.

This first wash was painted completely wet-into-wet. All the color was floating on the surface of the paper and was easily lifted to reveal a soft light color. I used tissue and a thirsty brush to lift in the areas where I wanted an atmospheric effect.

Karlyn Holman

The final darks were added on dry paper, and in some areas a fine spray of water was used to diffuse the color to keep the soft look. Waiting for the bus in France on a rainy day was not fun at the time, but the atmospheric feeling provided a good subject to paint.

# Lifting to capture energy and excitement

Water is a marvelous subject because this transparent liquid reflects light, creates dynamic contrasts and moves. Whether you are depicting a wet street scene or crashing waves, one of the best methods to capture this energy is to put the color down and then lift it away. The paper must be wet so the color will float on the surface and easily lift away. For this demonstration, I drew in some birds and masked them. then I wet the paper in every area except where I wanted little white, hard-edged shapes on the surface of the water. In this area, I threw water with my brush to create random wet and dry areas. The dry areas made the white shapes. I threw on the paint and lifted it away, simulating the movement of the crashing waves themselves. Using a tissue to lift the color revealed the soft whites underneath.

Lifting while the paint is wet takes a little patience because the color will try to return into the space. You are trying to coax the paint to be submissive to your desire, but the paint has a mind of its own. Just before the paint dries, try adding some table and popcorn salt for a sparkling effect.

Karlyn Holman

This finished painting was completed by using a razor blade to add additional sparkle, some Q-tips® to lift out some dried color, and a sponge to soften some areas. The masking was removed from the birds and the final details were added.

# Layering and glazing

In simple terms, layering or glazing is placing a wet color on top of a dry color. If the superimposed color is a harmonic color, you will create a jewel-like tone. If you use a complementary color, you will create a neutral tone. Transparent colors are optimal for glazing, but even opaque colors can be used. The color should be diluted with enough water to allow some of the undercolor to show through.

Layering or glazing can fulfill many functions. You can create **contrast** when you layer a dark over a light or a textured surface over a smooth surface, **change the temperature** when you layer cool over warm, or create a **concept** if you layer an image over an image. This technique adds dimension and perspective to your work.

Glazing is also an important tool used in correcting and finishing a painting. Sometimes your painting may have a flat or somewhat one-dimensional look. By glazing luminous washes over the surface in selected areas, you can achieve unity between the different elements of the painting and enrich the finished work. Glazing harmonic colors over your painting creates a pleasing glow much like the warm light created by a sunset.

When I noticed the suggestion of rock-like shapes in the abstract underpainting at the top of the page, I started to layer darker values of shapes in order to pull out the rock-like images. A series of unifying washes gave the finished painting a feeling of depth and shadow. Glazing gives you control because you can add more and more glazes until you get exactly the colors you want.

Karlyn Holman

# *Layering and glazing to create a strong light source*

This painting was inspired by the light source illuminating Grandpa Gary, Tyler and Jordan. Each face was purposefully interpreted by working warm to cool. First, I saved the white of the paper on the side of the faces illuminated by the light. I then used aureolin yellow, alizarin crimson and permanent magenta, working warm to cool, to create the feeling of a strong light source. After the faces were painted, I wet only the area behind the figures and applied a glaze of pure primaries starting with Winsor yellow, Winsor red and cobalt blue (warm to cool), allowing them to blend on the wet surface. After the local colors on the subjects were painted and had dried, I applied a glaze of permanent magenta and Antwerp blue to place the entire bottom half of the picture in darkness, creating an even more dramatic effect.

Layering is like telling a story. You set the scene with your underpainting and then you develop the characters in the succeeding layers. Finally, you add the hook—the darks.

# Layering to create a glow

**Jan Hartley** painted this glowing interpretation of leaves in a fall puddle by layering color wash over color wash. She started with a wet-into-wet underpainting, and each layer of darker color value added dimension and depth.

This style of layering is a traditional method of working in watercolor. Applying layer after layer of color over a dry surface can be a slow process, but it will create a glow that cannot be achieved by any other method. Using this technique is a good way to become better acquainted with the various qualities of each color. Staining, sedimentary, transparent or semi-transparent colors will all give varying results.

Jan painted this theme many times before she felt she had mastered the technique. Her determination resulted in a very unique painting.

A PUDDLE'S GOLDEN GIFT, Jan Hartley

# Layering to capture light and shadow

Layering color over color adds more energy and life to a painting than any other technique. This technique is the best way to depict light because layering color builds up luminosity and also adds depth and focus. Applying pure color over pure color, rather than layering mixed colors will build luminosity.

Light is energy. Trying to capture this energy on paper is quite an undertaking. This simple entryway in the quaint village of Tannenkirk, France, presented a wonderful study in the interplay of light and dark patterns. I was fascinated by the dramatic light of the cast shadows, the colors of the flowers, and the textures of the shingles and rocks. Trying to portray this mix of light and shadow was challenging.

The first layer was done on dry paper using the cool colors of cobalt and permanent magenta to capture the crisp cast shadows and the light bouncing around the subject.

This sketch was drawn with a Mars Stadler Graphic, # 313-7 sepia pen. I like the way the warm sepia tone blends with watercolor painting.

The foliage was created by literally throwing pure color into patterns of water. I used an Oriental brush to throw the water into patterns and then I threw in the colors of Winsor yellow, Antwerp blue and quinacridone burnt orange to make the greens, while at the same time, trying to accentuate the light side and shadow side.

The rocks were painted by wetting only the areas where the rock texture was desired and placing a warm and then a cool color onto the wet surface and letting these colors blend. After the color had a little time to soak into the paper, in order to create a rock-like texture, I placed a piece of wax paper on the color and left it there until it dried.

To finish the painting, I used harmonious warm colors such as raw sienna, scarlet lake and quinacridone burnt orange over the cool colors to create a glowing, luminous interpretation of the scene. As varying layers of paint were added, the white of the paper continued to reflect through the colors.

Karlyn Holman

# Layering for fun

In your search for new ideas, you need to play and let your intuitive skills experience free experimentation. This playtime is essential in order to discover new ideas and stimulate your imagination. Start with a wet-into-wet abstract underpainting of color, shape and movement using light- to mid-tone values. Think of this first layer as a work of art and enjoy every stroke, keeping color unity in mind as you move the color around. Use pure colors in this underpainting and remember that the only white is the white of the paper. Use a cold press paper so the layers of paint will not reactivate or disturb previous layers.

As the paint begins to settle into the paper, this is a good time to lift away some of the paint with a thirsty brush to regain some of the lights.

Now draw your ideas over this spontaneous underpainting. Shapes and movements created in the colors often suggest new elements for the composition. When entering this drawing stage, try to keep the same sense of spontaneity you used for the wet-into-wet wash. Artists who are gifted with intuitive design skills often draw directly with the paint and never use a pencil. Find the method that works for you.

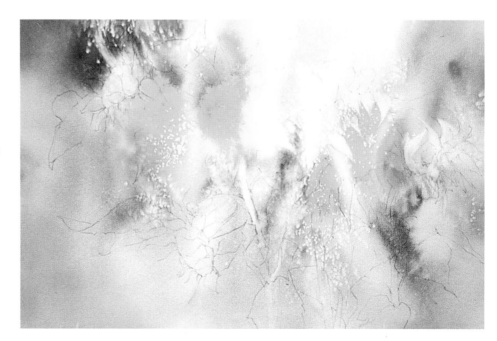

Now you are free to paint anything you desire over this dried underpainting. Using harmonic colors will add enrichment, while using complementary colors will add a neutralizing effect. Darks may be added in the final layering to accentuate your focal area.

In this particular painting, I realized that the final darks had lost some of the luminosity I was hoping to create, and the work was so full of hard edges that it needed something to soften the interpretation.

Using YES! paste thinned with water, I glued a piece of lightweight 10-gram white unryu over the painting, adding a veil of softness that could not be achieved with paint alone.

LAYERING AND GLAZING    109

# Layering to achieve luminosity

June Young's work goes way beyond recording her subject. She creates a visual statement reflecting an intense emotional response to her subject.

*June Young*

June Young loves to paint her compositions by layering color over color, working from light to dark. She always starts with the subject first and completes the background last. The first layer she paints is usually very light, and she works around the painting laying in washes of pale blue for cool areas and pale yellow and soft pink-reds for warm areas. She saves very little of the pure white of the paper.

This stage shows the soft underpainting of primary colors.

Layering more intense colors develops the glow radiating from within the hollyhocks.

Cool colors are added to create contrast.

*June Young*

The finished painting is a dramatic interpretation of full spectrum colors with glowing darks. The edges in the sunlit areas are kept soft, producing a warm glow. The dark background has a lost and found, out-of-focus quality, yet the edges touching the flowers provide a crisp contrast that accentuates the center of interest.

# Layering to create depth

June Young's style of painting does not provide instant gratification. When working on a painting, she has to maintain a level of emotional intensity similar to a marathon runner. This style of working at a sustained, prolonged pace reaps rewards such as the beautiful Yin and Yang of lost and found edges in this painting of berries.

The completed painting has a dark background for contrast. The overlapping planes and the softened edges create a **feeling of depth**, whereas the crisp in-focus edges appear to **come forward**.

This photograph shows only one of the many successive layers of paint June used to complete the painting.

# Layering to create richness and patina

Susan's paintings are deeply personal, semi-abstract interpretations of subjects she knows and loves. Each painting she creates goes beyond representation as she searches for new expressive territory.

*S. Luzier*

THE FISH AND THE FOWL, Susan Luzier

"If, as some say, a painting has a life of its own and I am its facilitator, then layering offers me a way to let that happen. When beginning a painting, I choose the technique and colors that feel appropriate for the mood I am in or the message that I wish to convey. For example, if I am feeling melancholy, I might make my first layer a loose and juicy wet-into-wet wash. Once this layer is dry and I have had a chance to study it, I rewet the paper and apply another layer of color. The story of the painting unfolds with each subsequent layer. Sometimes working on a painting is like reading a good book— I just do not want it to end. With each layer, the painting surface increases in richness, poetry, mystery and personal involvement. The creative process has pushed me into new confrontations in my work. Layering challenges me to discover and enhance relationships of color, shape and value, and to use all the elements and principles of good design. When I paint, I try to be patient and develop a relationship with the painting, knowing that sometimes I must accept the unexpected quirks of personality that evolve with each work. Layering helps me to trust my intuition and let my inner voice guide me. By not perceiving an outcome at the start, I free myself to be a facilitator, to listen for guidance, to respond to the activity of each layer, and to allow the painting to truly have a life of its own.

"THE FISH AND THE FOWL is from my *Fossil* series that honors life from a different time on our planet.

"GEISHA IN HER GARDEN began as layer upon layer, when suddenly the Geisha appeared. She makes me smile every time I look at this painting."

GEISHA IN HER GARDEN, Susan Luzier

EACH HEART IS A PILGRIM, Susan Luzier

LAS FLORES DE LAGUNA NIGUEL, Susan Luzier

"EACH HEART IS A PILGRIM is a layered painting that speaks to something which I am passionate about—each person's need to have a direct relationship with the Divine. This heart is so filled with love that it is spilling over with blossoms of flowers.

"LAS FLORES DE LAGUNA NIGUEL is the California bougainvilleas that are made all the more brilliant by layering color over color."

"Developing your own personal style is more important than mastering techniques. With time, practice and patience, you will begin to zero in on your content and message and your personal style will begin to evolve. I encourage my students to paint in the way that is the least effortful for them, as this is their most natural expression. I urge them to pay attention to any shapes, symbols or gestures that show up repeatedly in their work and consider using them as themes. I also advise students to limit their workshop exposure and to concentrate on working in their own studios without outside influences and distractions. We must all be accepting of who and where we are in our artistic journey.

"Finally, I suggest that we take our lives as artisans out of the studio and into all the moments of our day. Through consciousness, we can inject creative awareness and sacredness in all we do, no matter how small or mundane the task."

# Lost and found edges

Lost and found edges comprise the magic element that gives your painting variety. Your paintings will be more interesting if you build in mysterious or undelineated elements that the viewer must interpret. If all your edges are hard, your painting could become boring. There is no magic formula for how many lost or found edges are necessary for a successful painting. Intuition will guide you as you gain more mastery over this technique.

There are several ways to lose edges. One effective way is to paint the same values next to each other. Another is to soften the painted edge with water while it is still wet by using a damp brush or a fine mister. Many lost edges and equal value edges were formed in this wet-into-wet underpainting, as illustrated by this black and white and color interpretation of the same subject.

The soft edges of the cats were fused with the background mass, and the colors were allowed to flow into the foreground shadows. Aerial perspective was achieved by keeping the background soft to create a feeling of depth. Lineal perspective was achieved by suggesting some receding floor tiles as they diminished into the background.

The painting was finished on dry paper by adding some crisp edges in the center of interest. If you need to soften more edges after the paint dries, use a damp, stiff brush or a damp Q-tip®.

Keep in mind that if all the edges in this painting were crisp, they would draw too much attention and tend to flatten the shapes of the cats. Hard edges stop the eye from moving through the painting. By adding some soft or lost edges, you add depth to the painting and allow the viewer's eye to move behind or around your subject. You may choose to use more hard edges in your center of interest, but adding some undefined edges will soften your work and add more interest and balance to your painting.

# Creating a focus area using lost and found edges

When painting portraits, take the time and effort to sharpen your drawing skills, especially if you want a likeness. You may want to start with photographs because they allow you time to study the subject in depth. I used several photographs taken in full sunlight to define the important cast shadows on Rachael's face.

My main goal in this wet-into-wet underpainting was to create a variety of mostly soft edges so Rachael's features would be the most expressive element in the painting, and her hair and clothing would diffuse into the background. I wanted to create a feeling of mystery and playfulness. By keeping some edges crisp and others soft, I was able to accent the cast light on Rachael's features. Values and patterns in the areas of shadow are established in this first high-energy step. I used new gamboges and alizarin crimson to establish her skin tone, letting the edges melt into the hair. For the blond hair, I used raw sienna and quinacridone gold and then layered permanent magenta over the yellows and allowed the paint to mix on the paper into a neutral gray.

Karlyn Holman

The successive layers were completed on dry paper to allow more control. My biggest challenge was deciding where to create hard edges without undoing the feeling of softness. Every painting is a learning experience. Why don't you try your hand at portraiture—it is a very challenging and satisfying subject.

# Adding emotional impact using lost and found edges

Using an abstract motif is a marvelous way to practice creating lost and found edges and produces a painting that is expressive in its emotional content. When you are creating abstract art, you are working with the basic elements of design and color theory, but you are not limited to rendering an accurate representation.

Lost edges in a painting direct the viewer through the painting. The shapes can be simple such as round or rectilinear. You can create lost and found edges and reversals with just a little pre-planning and then let everything go full speed ahead.

Karlyn Holman

118

This wet-into-wet start was created by simply applying rich color next to rich color and adding textural agents, such as Thai white unryu paper, gauze and plastic wrap.

The gauze and plastic wrap were removed, but the unryu paper was glued down exactly where it was placed in the underpainting using YES! paste mixed with water.

Karlyn Holman

The circles and rectangles were drawn directly on the surface with pencil. The main focus was to enjoy painting crisp, found edges in some areas and losing edges in other areas. Always look at the *big picture* when creating lost and found edges so you can create light and dark paths that connect throughout the painting. For example, notice how the vertical shape is dark against a light background at the top and then the same shape transposes into light against a dark background at the bottom.

# Negative painting

Positive and negative shapes are not always black and white, nor are they necessarily the shapes that surround your subjects. As your painting evolves, the difference between negative and positive shapes becomes more difficult to define.

Developing a balance of both negative and positive areas will add depth and a sense of balance and integrity to your painting. Blending the background with your subject, or blending one shape into another will add variety to the composition. In transparent watercolor, working in positive and negative shapes is extremely important because you do not use white or opaque color. As you work more and more with transparent watercolor, you will intuit this relationship of positive and negative elements.

These two paintings by **Judy Blain** show a completely dark and completely light background. If you analyze these paintings carefully, you will see why Judy is a master of negative painting.

AFTERNOON PEONIES, Judy Blain

ZINNIA GARDEN, Judy Blain

120

# Negative painting as an easy, direct approach

This approach separates the subject into two positive layers of direct painting. First, you draw and paint the subject on dry paper and then mask over the painted image. Next, you simply paint the wet-into-wet wash over your masked subject and this becomes your negative background. This layered approach does not require tedious painting around the shapes and results in a fresh, spontaneous look. The masked flowers become the positive shapes and the soft, blurred background becomes the negative shape. This approach is usually a successful method for beginners, as well as advanced painters, and often results in a polished painting.

Karlyn Holman

# Creating a shape within a shape

Superimposing a shape over a shape is a challenging technique to try. Drawing and planning beforehand will help avoid possible problems and free you to paint with abandon. Research your subject and look for contrast and daring new angles. The subject of flowers is popular with most watercolor artists. Even though I have painted flowers many times, I still approach every composition with a renewed sense of determination to make the new interpretation my best. What little twist can I try that will be new? What combination of colors haven't I tried before? Painting a familiar subject is like spending time with an old friend. We feel reassured and accepted, but at the same time, we can be stimulated and surprised.

These calla lilies have simple, dynamic shapes that provide a great contrast to the dark, warm background.

Karlyn Holman

This painting is a combination of some masked and some directly painted flowers. The multi-petaled, light flowers were masked before the background was painted. The red flowers were painted after the background was completed. Notice how the dark poppy has a light background and the light flowers have a dark background. Keep this reversal in mind when planning your composition.

Karlyn Holman

Morning glories are a perfect subject for this "break out" concept because of the way the foliage intertwines and curls. Simply let the vines curl onto the edges of the paper. When these paintings are completed, they are put into frames with all of the white space showing. Allowing the leaves or vines to pass through the white space and touch the edges of the paper gives the painting more integrity.

In this painting of wildflowers, the grasses were painted directly on the mat. These paintings are popular with interior designers, who often use them to add a unique touch to their decorating schemes.

# Mixing negative and positive shapes in one alla prima approach

This approach is more challenging because you are constantly painting around the shapes, as well as painting the shapes themselves. As you add color, you may find it difficult to distinguish between the negative and positive shapes. Making an effort to experiment with both positive and negative shapes at the same time will add depth and balance to your paintings, and, most importantly, will give you the satisfaction of being able to control an *alla prima* approach to negative painting.

I have found that an excellent way to experience negative painting is to use the Masa paper technique. This archival Japanese paper fractures the color into beautiful networks of lines and softly blends the colors. Painting on regular watercolor paper can be very hard-edged, whereas the use of Masa paper allows control, while producing a fluidity and movement that is very exciting. You can sketch ahead of time or draw with the paint directly on your paper. Any intuitive approach can be risky, but you will find it can reap great rewards.

The following procedure is not the traditional way to approach this technique. Instead of painting first and gluing later, I like to get the gluing out of the way so the creative process is not interrupted.

Start by marking an "X" on the smooth side of the paper. Crumple the Masa paper and soak it in clean water.

Open it very carefully and place the paper with the "X" up on a piece of watercolor paper. Carefully lift the paper back to the halfway point and place glue on the watercolor paper.

Place the Masa on top of the glued surface and roll a brayer over the papers. I prefer to use YES! paste, thinned with water. Repeat this procedure on the other half of the paper.

You must paint on this surface before the paper dries in order to create the batik-like fractures.

Paint the subject as well as around the subject—enjoy the freedom and excitement of watching the colors magically create varying textures. When the painting is dry, you may decide to add more crisp edges.

Karlyn Holman

# Approaching negative painting intuitively— dancing with paint

Bonnie listens to her intuitive voice, and this trust in her inner self allows her to paint in an improvisational approach, allowing the colors and shapes to evolve into a finished painting.

*Bonnie Broitzman*

"Since childhood, each of us have been making positive marks on paper. Thinking of those marks as 'positive painting' leaves the empty space around such marks as the negative space. The negative is really the space not used by the strokes of the artist's brush. Painting is an opportunity to dance, shaping the negative space, as well as the positive marks. When intuitively using a stroke, here and then there, the artist comes as close to a real dance on paper as I believe a visual artist can experience. In a successful watercolor, a wonderful balance arises when the artist leaps between the negative and the positive areas. It is as beautiful as witnessing the graceful leaps of professional dancers across a stage. The viewer can experience a similar joy and excitement by allowing his or her eyes to dance from one area to another, as the artist did during the act of creation. Because it is shared with an audience, the creative process is complete."

PAINTING AS PRAYER, Bonnie Broitzman

EARTH DANCE: SEA TO SEE, Bonnie Broitzman

PAINTING AS PRAYER. "I began to wonder what prayer would look like if it were in color, line and shape, instead of words. I quietly began to add color to very wet paper, giving it a *caught in the moment between time and space feeling*; my twenty-minute morning meditation gave visual form to the elemental energy of color and shape."

EARTH DANCE: SEA TO SEE. "During this intuitive painting demonstration, my college students recognized a Georgia O'Keefe skull. A moment later, the skull had transformed into a dancing female figure. Such is the joy and surprise of starting a painting with no preconceived idea or pencil lines."

RECAPTURED LIGHT. "This painting was a gift of my longtime friendship with Karlyn. The events of my life shrouded my watercolor papers in almost total darkness. Karlyn encouraged me to find some 'lights' and some 'rest' places. I took the painting to her sink, washing layers of darkness away. It took only a few positive strokes to discover its unique beauty."

The following journal entry *Follow Your Bliss*, dated February 14, 2001, is in response to the question "Why did you become a visual artist?"

"My journey as artist, evolved slowly. My soul crawled through the night, swelling like a seed, until its hard, stationary exterior shell cracked! Exposed like a chick penetrating its shell, life had exhausted me. I needed care and nurturing.

"I lived a double life: sneaking into my basement studio, not waking my sleeping family, to study. Painting and drawing in absolute quiet, I pecked away at the norms that had framed my exterior life. As wife, mother and teacher, I did my daytime exterior work, but it was this emerging night work that began to shape a new creative, interior life.

"Stronger, clearer, I shared my fledgling art with a few other artists and I was accepted and encouraged among others of my own kind. We were birthing new lives not filled with diapers or dishes, but abundant with flowing images, glowing on white paper. Abstracted landscapes, flowers,

fruits and vegetables danced with pure color and line, expressing a more elemental life, one of color, line, shape and harmony. Collectively we experienced a joy and a lust for art that saturated our conversations with images and terms from a much larger world. Times painting together were reminiscent of quilting circles from an earlier time, but perhaps they laced a larger image. As educated women, we were capable of caring far beyond the borders of our immediate families. We patched together a vision not meant to warm just one family, in one location, but to blanket a larger world. As changing women, we were open to all colors and a larger world of love, joy and peace.

"Come! The invitation to this feast is open to everyone to co-create, between Father Sky and Mother Earth. Together we can celebrate each birth, for we are all part of a larger world that awaits the crack of each shell, allowing the great earth energy to color our lives beautifully."

# Structured realism

## Joye Moon

"The mere words, negative painting, sound frightening and unattainable to most artists. Through the years, I have tried to simplify this process for my students by referring to this technique as 'just painting the background stuff.' For some reason, this lifts the burden from them so they can move forward unafraid.

"I like to vary the background shapes as much as possible to create more diversity in the painting. Some areas may be flat washes of color that gently define the edge of a flower petal or a branch of leaves. Other areas may appear very organic with a textural quality. I use negative painting to interpret abstract subject matter as well as structured realism because it adds depth and dimension to the two-dimensional surface. Negative painting also adds character and mystery, and while the technique can be challenging, experimenting with it can be fun.

A WINDY DAY, Joye Moon

"In the painting A WINDY DAY, I developed many different types of negative areas to make the flowers come alive. Starting with no preconceived idea, I introduced paint onto a wet paper surface. (I like to use 140# Winsor Newton cold press). At that point, I was only thinking about color, shape and movement. While the paint was still wet, I lightly sprinkled Epsom salt, table salt, popcorn salt and drops of alcohol on the surface. I also placed plastic wrap on the top left side of the painting and some gauze on the lower left, applying more paint on top of the gauze to ensure a good transfer of color. After this phase dried, I removed the plastic wrap and gauze. At this stage, the entire painting was completely soft-edged. Next, I began to develop the flowers and leaf shapes by painting in the background only. Instead of penciling any imagery on the paper, I used my intuition as the composition developed, using negative painting to describe the positive shapes. I visualized the shapes of the flowers and proceeded to add color around the edges and into the background, striving to avoid merely outlining the flowers. An interesting bold color background shape created more depth and interest. The flowers you see came to life as a result of using the technique of negative painting."

PEEKABOO, Joye Moon

"The painting, PEEKABOO, began with a well-defined drawing of tulips. Masking fluid was applied in several key areas to conserve the white of the paper. Although this composition is structured realism and looks like a traditional direct painting, I actually used many negative shapes to achieve the final composition.

Negative painting is not an impossible concept to grasp. By experimenting with the use of negative shapes and gradually incorporating them into your paintings, the techniques should become easier. You will soon be able to visualize the positive shapes by emphasizing the negative shapes. This black and white copy dramatically visualizes the reversal of the PEEKABOO tulips.

# Improvisation with control

## BRIDGET AUSTIN

Bridget is an expert at juggling improvisation with control. She begins her paintings using a free-flowing, fluid technique and then masterfully uses controlled, crisp, hard-edged shapes to achieve her expressive interpretations of her subjects.

"I think anyone who wishes to create has to find the media that suits his or her temperament, skills and subjects—the perfect vehicle. For me, transparent watercolor using negative painting is pure joy. First, of course, comes the inspiration— the moment in time to be shared. Then, I organize my impressions in a very basic value sketch—just enough information to know where the light and dark areas are to be and how the page will be broken up. This sketch is often very abstract. Next, comes the excitement of putting paint and water on the paper—lots of paint and lots of water!—and watching it flow and settle in always unique ways. This method allows water media to act like water media—it flows! Sometimes I wet the entire paper, and sometimes I work on dry paper, and introduce water and paint to specific hard-edged sections. I then analyze the results and using my sketch, I begin to develop values by applying layers of paint before focusing on details. I often work light to dark, but in some cases I reverse the process. The middle stages of the painting often require hope and vision, but when I begin adding smaller, more specific shapes, things start to look up! There are usually at least three layers of paint in some areas, and as I chisel away at the shape edges, I find such pleasure and challenge in revealing the interesting shapes that eventually make the puzzle come together. Easy to start, hard to finish—maybe! But how fascinating to watch the painting unfold."

BASKING IN THE MORNING SUN. "Some subjects just beg to be painted. In this painting, I tried to capture the beautiful morning light highlighting the colors of the flowers against the dramatic dark background. This painting was pure pleasure to do. The initial wash was painted with one- and two-inch flat brushes on dry hot-pressed board, leaving some crisp whites, but resulting in a continuous flow of color in a rainbow-like ribbon throughout the painting. I knew where the roses were but did not need to identify specific flowers at this point. The beauty in this approach is that the painting is already tied together from the beginning. In the second layer, I found some of the edges and details of the flowers and leaves. When that layer dried, I returned to the areas that needed some extra emphasis and detail, keeping in mind how the light and dark patterns provide movement through the painting. Try to resist finding too many details—you will soon learn to recognize when less is more. In this case, I wanted to suggest light in a garden and keep some of the fresh feeling that the scene gave me, rather than find every leaf or stem."

SUMMER LAKESIDE. "What fascinating places rock ledges are! This particular one seemed a special treat, with pure highlights, interesting shapes, and the stark contrast of values, as well as the lacy wildflowers against the massive rock formation. I wanted to spend more time here and was able to do so through my painting. This painting was more structured than some that I do, as there is a sky and distant tree line, but the treatment of the rocks and flowers provides the center of interest. On dry Lana 300# cold press paper, I created a shape that encompassed all the rocks, grasses and flowers. The color of the rocks flowed into the grass and bushes. I used tissue to enhance the texture of the rocks and leaves. When this area dried, I isolated and defined the different elements of the composition by painting up to the edges of the shapes. I tried to maintain the continuity of the painting by allowing the light and dark areas to flow into each other, using several layers of paint to achieve this goal. By using negative painting techniques, I was able to discover all of the small joys of this beautiful place."

*Summer Lakeside, Bridget Austin*

AUTUMN LEAVES TAPESTRY. "This painting elevates any square foot of forest floor to a worthy—and challenging—subject. Okay, I admit I was careful to select an interesting square foot or so, as the types and sizes of the leaves are quite varied. In this case, I did not leave any pure white sparkling paper. This is a decision I did not make lightly, but this subject called for a softer, more subdued treatment and colors. The entire page was wet, and color was introduced. When the paint was dry, I developed shapes by painting around interesting areas. Some areas have many layers of paint, others only two. Not every leaf is defined, creating a sense of mystery which encourages the viewer to *finish* the painting visually."

*Autumn Tapestry, Bridget Austin*

ON THE WATER. "This painting celebrates one of life's small pleasures—some fall leaves temporarily floating on a pond, soon to sink to the bottom. The rock areas were painted simply in order to maintain the contrast between the white stone and the murky pond and colored leaves. The colors for the leaves and water were applied at the same time to create an underpainting of textures for the leaves. I layered the dark of the pond over the initial color and painted up to and around the leaves. By applying another layer of paint, I discovered the rocks at the bottom of the pond and added just enough details to the leaves to capture the essence of the scene."

*On the Water, Bridget Austin*

# Liquid frisket

Liquid frisket is a rubbery substance used to preserve the white of the paper and areas of color. This material comes in many colors and has many names—miskit, resist, maskoid and white mask, to name a few. I prefer using a white mask because it goes on white and dries clear which has the advantage of letting you see the actual color you are using and not the color of the frisket. You can paint or spatter it on with a brush or a painting knife. Once the liquid frisket is dry, you can freely paint, knowing the masked areas are protected. After the paint dries, you can remove the frisket with your fingers or with a rubber cement pick-up. You must be careful to select a paper that holds the color, such as Arches cold press, because softer paper may result in the loss of color when you remove the frisket. Softer paper may also lose some of its surface.

This quick value study interprets the drawing as three simple values—light, mid-tone and dark.

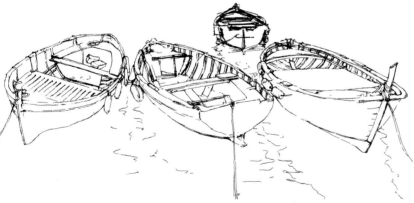

Using several photographs, I drew these shapes of old world boats in Portovenere, Italy. On the day I photographed these boats, the light was constantly changing and at times, was blinding as it bounced off the water. In order to capture the crisp edges of the boats and the intense sun penetrating from above, I carefully chose the areas I wanted to remain white. After applying the frisket, I was free to paint with abandon because the whites were protected.

I painted the cast shadows on the boats and in the water using only cobalt blue and permanent magenta.

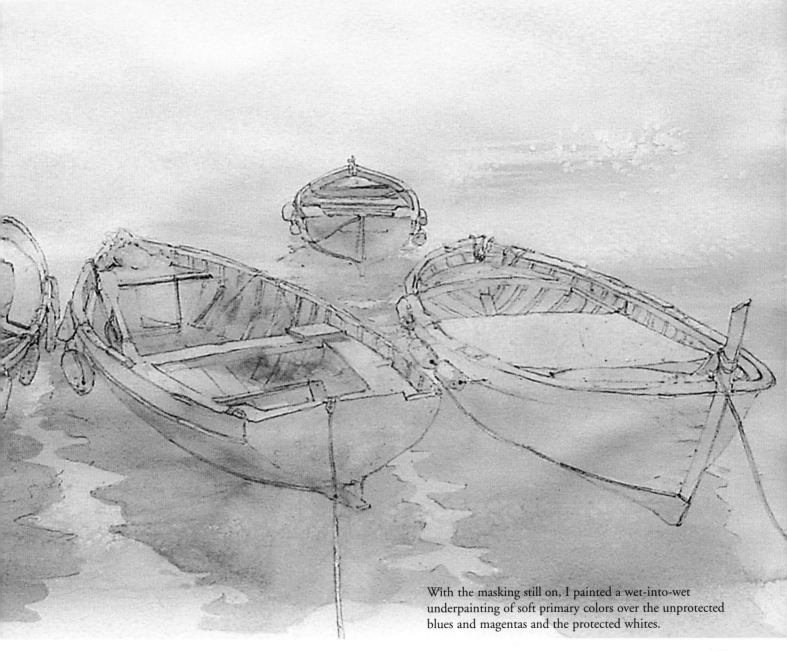

With the masking still on, I painted a wet-into-wet underpainting of soft primary colors over the unprotected blues and magentas and the protected whites.

This step shows the local color added to the boats
and the dark values added to the water.

The last step was to mask one more time over the areas I wanted to protect, and paint a more intense, unifying wash of colors over the entire work. Masking almost always creates some edges that are too hard. To soften a few of those edges, simply use a stiff oil painter's brush dipped in water.

# Drawing with frisket

A palette knife was used to apply the liquid frisket in this painting. To use this technique, dip the knife or a stick in the masking fluid and use it like a drawing implement. Using a knife produces very crisp and slick lines. When you have completed drawing with the mask, you can also spatter on some white spots. To clean up, simply wipe the blade with a tissue.

This photograph by **Ilona Fellows** shows the playful patterns of light on a sea turtle. Masking was used to define the movement of the light in the water and the descriptive lines on the turtle shell and body. I randomly applied masking to the outside lines of the turtle, which allowed some of the color applied to the turtle to seep into water, thereby creating the look of refracted light.

After allowing the masking to dry, I wet the entire paper and freely splashed the color on the turtle and in the water. Pure primary colors were applied and allowed to mix on the paper. Every blue on my palette was used to achieve harmonic depth and a value change from dark to light in the water. This painting experience is similar to the batik process.

More masking was applied over the dried color to produce the patterns of movement in the water above the turtle.

Darker values of blues and violets were added to enhance the masked pattern of movement in the water. Darker colors were used to define the turtle.

Karlyn Holman

More masked lines of movement were added in the foreground, and another layer of blues and violets was applied. I removed the masking on the turtle and layered some cobalt shadows over parts of the turtle so he appeared to be underwater. More blues were layered over the new masked areas to capture the playful patterns of light. When the painting was dry, any areas that were too crisp were softened with color or by using a damp, stiff brush to blur the edges.

# Working with a painting knife and unconventional tools

A favorite technique used by oil painters is to build up thick, impasto surfaces using a painting knife. I particularly enjoyed using this method when painting in oils and was thrilled to find out that you can also use a painting knife to create marvelous lines and textural shapes in watercolor. You can draw with your knife by scooping up a richly pigmented mixture of paint on one edge of the knife and use the tip of the knife like an ink pen. By flicking the tip of the flexible blade loaded with paint, you can create spatters.

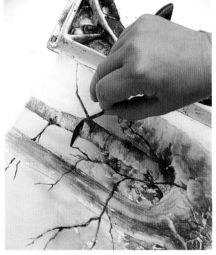

The painting knife was used to draw the branches, to apply paint on the birch tree and branches, and to flick the burnt sienna spots on the birch tree.

**Marie Findlay** painted this semi-abstract, whimsical interpretation of a family by wetting the paper, stretching plastic wrap into face shapes, puncturing holes for the features and using gauze to suggest the hair. She created this painting for her son, a psychologist, who not only works with "fractured" families, but has a fractured family of his own, made up of "his, hers and theirs."

138

Joyce Gow

A credit card, a stiff piece of cardboard or a rubber spatula may be the tool you are looking for. Joyce Gow discovered this technique while teaching a workshop in Florida. Using a credit card edge, she was able to duplicate the image of roses that a student had brought from her garden. In a subsequent class, she tried using a spatula belonging to one of her students and it worked perfectly. She often uses these unconventional tools in creating her exquisite floral paintings.

This beautiful painting was done using a spatula. If the moisture of the paint is at the right dampness, the spatula acts like a squeegee and leaves an edge of paint that duplicates a shadow area. Another technique Joyce used in this painting was to pick up thick paint with a palette knife and literally draw the stems and leaves with this tool. Finally, she used a drinking straw to blow the wet paint on the stems, creating the suggestion of thorns.

# Creating textures

Texture is both a design element and a technique. There are as many ways to create texture as there are ways to paint pictures. The following descriptions explain a few of the more popular methods.

## Spattering

Spattering is a habit-forming technique. I cannot resist blessing my work with a few flicks of paint either spattered off my brush or flicked off my painting knife. You can also spatter liquid maskoid to create light spatters or white ink to create snow.

## Adding salt to wet paint

Salt comes in various grades including fine popcorn, table, Epsom, rock and kosher. Salt creates a granular texture when dropped onto a wet surface. The salt actually repels the water and leaves a white shape that varies in size depending on the size of the original salt particle and the degree of dampness of the paper. If you add the salt when the surface is extremely wet, you will create a soft, dissolved look. Most artists choose to add salt when the shine is almost leaving the paper in order to achieve a distinct white shape. By adding salt, you can suggest a mysterious, soft wintry effect, the texture of animal fur or even the illusion of rushing water. The use of salt is controversial and falls in and out of favor with artists and museums. Salt leaves a residue when it dries that could affect the permanence of color. During times of high humidity, the salt may even reactivate and continue to dissolve the paint. Many artists avoid salt for these reasons.

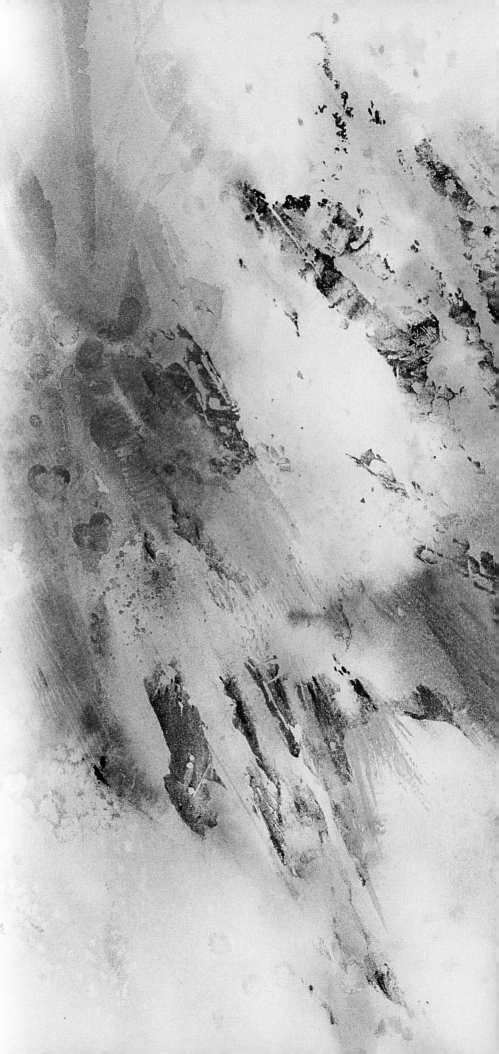

## Adding alcohol to the wet surface

Like salt, rubbing alcohol repels water as it wicks into the paper, creating a whimsical, soft bubble-shaped texture. Alcohol is so unpredictable that if allowed to penetrate the paper, it may create dark value shapes. It can be applied by dripping, spraying or painting. You can produce a marvelous line by squeezing the alcohol out of a bottle with a needle on the top. A pen tip, cotton swabs or almost any tool you can devise will work. If you choose to experiment with alcohol, be sure to read the warnings on the container. A well-ventilated work area is essential because the fumes can be dangerous.

## Dry Brush

Dry brush technique is a very popular effect that is most easily accomplished on rough or cold-pressed paper. By simply using less water and more paint as you glide the bristles over the surface, you can create a broken, grainy look. This technique is often used to simulate weathered wood or old buildings.

## Nontraditional tools

Remember that not all of your tools have to come from an artist supply house. Nonporous plastic wrap, gauze, charcoal, paper clips, mesh bags, stencils, rubber stamps—all of these materials can be used to create unique effects.

# Stamping and stenciling

The more we grow as artists, the more we can appreciate semi-abstraction. This particular demonstration illustrates a simple, direct approach to designing space and creating textures that capture the essence of the subject. The less detail or rendering you put into your painting, the more interpretation you leave up to the viewer. The techniques used for this lesson are extremely simple, yet very effective. Stamping, stenciling and cutting shapes are reminiscent of grade school days—a return to the playful child within each of us.

After spending several weeks in the vineyards in the Alsace-Lorraine region of France, I could not resist painting an interpretation of the grapes at their peak of perfection. One day while we were driving through the lush countryside, we actually made our bus driver stop so we could photograph the vineyards and pick some leaves to use as stencils.

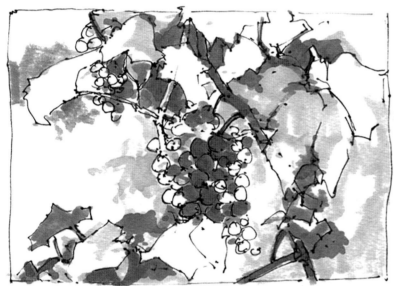

This value study was done using 40% and 60% value pens to establish a semi-abstract composition.

Wet the paper on both sides and apply light, pure colors in harmonic overtones. You are not painting the subject yet; you are only capturing the essence of the light values in an underpainting. To interpret the purple grapes, cut grape-sized circles out of wax paper and place some on the light value paper. Continue painting deeper values of color and adding more circles. By adding the circles at intervals, you will capture the light hitting the subject and achieve more variations in color interpretation.

Try using the back of actual grape leaves to apply the pure colors of yellow and blue, adding a touch of the complementary color. When you **stamp** the leaves on the paper, the colors will mix together in an unpredictable way. Do not remove the leaves. Let them remain on the paper to use as **stencils** by painting around them. Use gauze to suggest some trailing vines, paint in some mid-tone darks and wait for everything to dry.

Now comes the most exciting part! Remove the leaves and wax paper, unveiling the textures you have created.

Karlyn Holman

Use your intuition to complete the painting. Adding a few darks and a few negative shapes will usually pull the painting together. If you cut grape-sized circles out of a piece of acetate, you can lift some light-toned grape shapes with a damp sponge. This lesson is great for sharpening your negative painting skills. The final painting allows great freedom in interpretation and imagination, both for the artist and the viewer. The unintentional bits of inspiration that happen, combined with your intuitive touches, usually make semi-abstract painting a joyful experience.

# Adding more texture with plastic wrap and gauze

This painting shows a variation of the same process as outlined on the previous pages. For this painting, I placed plastic wrap and gauze on the wet paint to add more textures. Twisting the gauze results in great grape tendrils. While the paint was still wet, I applied metallic gold spray paint in selected areas and allowed the paint to dry. After adding the negative darks to finish the painting, I added gold webbing spray to achieve the whimsical, unexpected line that this spray produces.

Karlyn Holman

144

# Using wax paper as a stamp

Wax paper is a marvelous shape maker. By cutting, folding or ripping wax paper, you can create a myriad of effects. Try cutting out acorn shapes and combining them with oak leaves or gather fall leaves for use as stamps and make them look like they are floating in a puddle of water. You can create just about anything you can imagine. Simply prepare your wax paper shapes and place them on a wet surface. Add color and let the color seep under and around the wax paper. You can also add more shapes on the wet color and watch the color wick around the shapes. Leave the wax paper on until it dries.

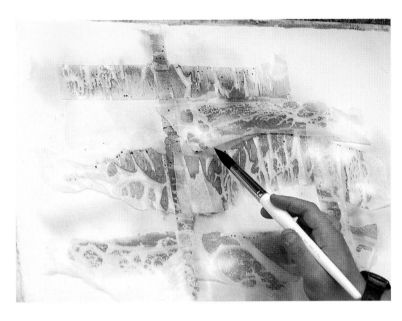

This semi-abstract painting was inspired by my impressions of Japan. I tried to imply a feeling of formality by imposing the lattice-like vertical and horizontal shapes. Folding wax paper in an accordion style shape and applying color on and around the wax paper shape created the bridge.

Karlyn Holman

This demonstration has all the texturing agents removed from the surface. The remaining painting is still considered a transparent watercolor, because none of these agents remain on the surface.

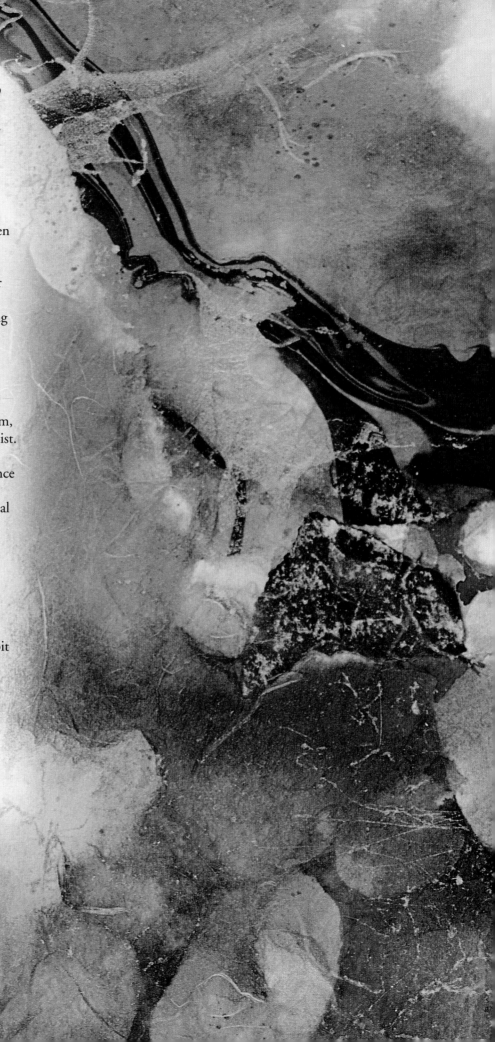

## CHAPTER FOUR

# Staying on the path by seeking new adventures

One of your best sources of inspiration may be that panicky feeling you get when you face a blank sheet of paper. This pre-painting tension creates energy and is often the catalyst that transforms your anxiety into inspiration. Even if you are not sure of yourself, try to put something fresh and new into every painting. Inspiration can be greatly enhanced when you abandon the safe path and decide to take risks.

Watercolor, more than any other medium, really expresses the personality of the artist. The techniques are so varied that every artistic personality can find its voice. Once you have mastered the techniques, your biggest hurdle to expressing your personal vision is to stay inspired. The following ideas are suggestions to help you in this endeavor.

As your paintings evolve, you must find time to reflect on your progress and to critique your work. Eventually, I would encourage you to participate in an exhibit or hold an open house to show your paintings, which will allow you to evaluate your work by seeing it in a new environment. This is the time for you to reflect and celebrate and share your work with others. Looking at your work from this new perspective may influence the path you take next.

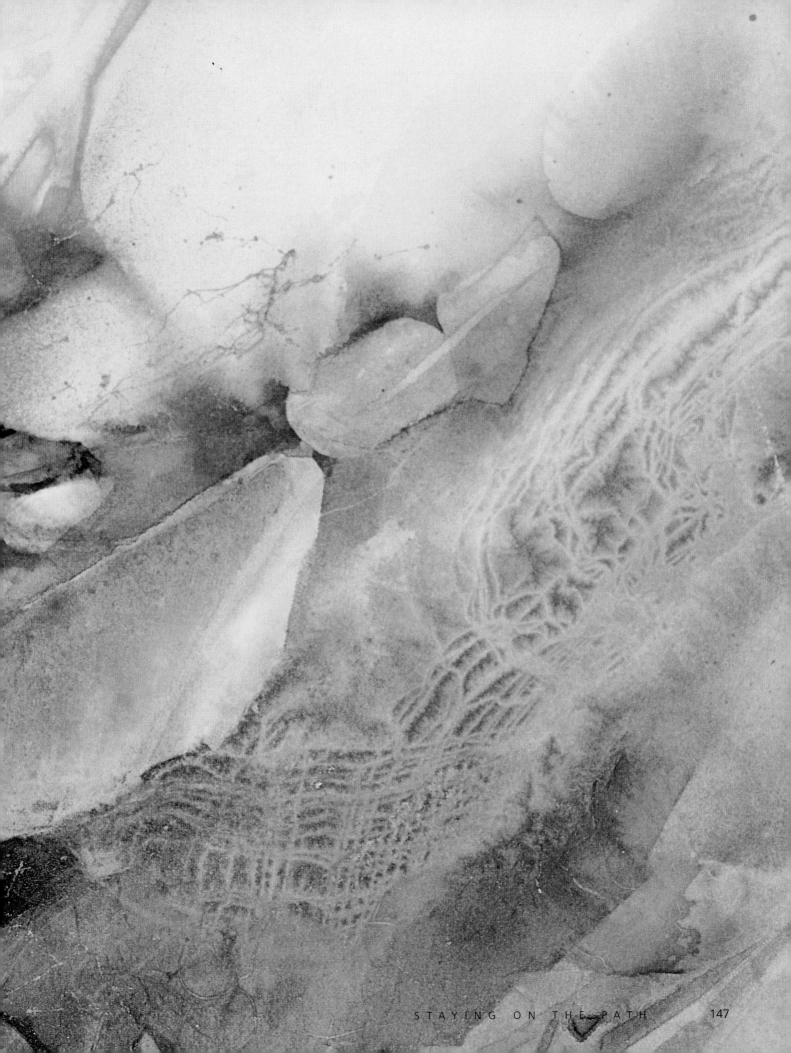

# Consider working in a series

Subjects often choose me. Living by Lake Superior for so many years has given me a great appreciation for such simple forms as rocks. Rock images started a whole series of paintings that will continue to inspire me for many years. Working in a series allows you to express your subject in more depth and may give you additional insight into how your work is evolving. When you work in a series, you become more and more connected with the subject. As you move from painting to painting, ideas evolve from your previous work. You begin to explore new spatial relationships, new color combinations, variations in textures, and numerous subtle changes achieved only by sustained concentration on your subject.

When you paint the same subject over and over again, you will find yourself doing less recording and more discovering. The familiarity you experience by working with the same subject often helps you move in a new direction. This new vision could be from realism to a more abstract style, or from a traditional approach to a more interpretive style.

This painting, BOXED-IN ROCKS, was created by designing simple, rectilinear shapes with a pencil and then painting along the lines to create crisp edges.

BOXED-IN ROCKS, Karlyn Holman

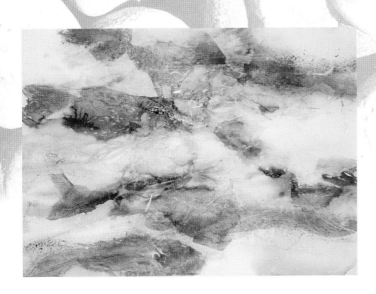

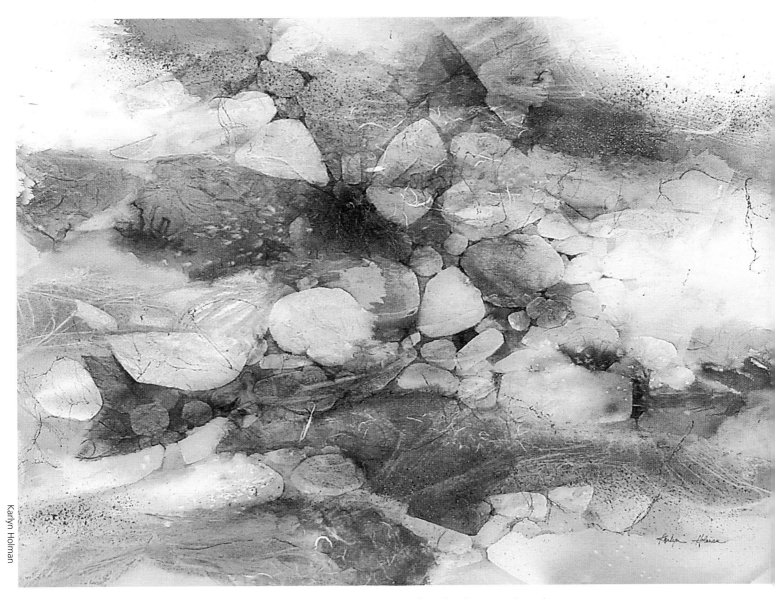

This abstract start had the suggestion of rocks in some of the shapes. I decided to make a number of semi-abstract shapes by negatively painting in selected areas. To reach the final interpretation, I used washes of cool colors in selected areas to make some of the rocks appear to be underwater. The hardest part was to not go too far and to leave some of the interpretation up to the viewer.

# Unearth your buried treasure

As your stack of unresolved paintings rises to new heights, challenge yourself to save these paintings by any possible means. Try anything and everything in an attempt to unearth the buried treasure in these unresolved paintings and transform them into a new reality.

Almost every painting has some good elements that are worth saving—the key to this search is to rip out the parts of your painting that you like and place them on a new ground. This takes great courage and open-mindedness, but in no time you will be tearing and gluing and seeing results. Glue the pieces down with any glue that is designed for gluing paper to paper. I prefer YES! paste.

Add collage paper to enrich the surface or continue painting and let new life flow into the composition. Enjoy this free-flowing playtime and let your intuition guide you.

Here, the ripped up painting has been redesigned onto a new surface.

More collage paper was glued down to add harmonic enrichment and to form connecting elements that add unity to the painting.

Karlyn Holman

The entire surface is then wet and more color is applied. The new interpretation will now be judged on design and content. You have unearthed the key elements of color, value, texture and shape and interpreted them with a new integrity.

# Carry a camera with you at all times

A camera translates subjects differently than our minds eye. Oftentimes, our memory of a subject is totally different than what our photographs show. Sometimes our photographs are more inspiring than our memory of the image. I usually use my camera as a tool to record the light and freeze a subject for future reference, but I am surprised time after time when the camera captures a point of view and a sensitivity that my mind's eye missed. Never apologize for using a camera—it is an indispensable tool. In these busy times, photographs may be a substitute for the luxury of spending hours sketching or painting on location.

If you carry a camera with you at all times, you can visually evaluate potential subjects anytime, anywhere. Train yourself to be open to these possibilities by observing everything around you. These intuitive glimpses through the camera lens may produce surprising sources of inspiration.

My husband, Gary, snapped this photo of the New York skyline as we were leaving the harbor. The backlighting produced a remarkable photo, even more beautiful than our memory of the event.

Barbara McFarland snapped this photograph in the historic city of San Miguel de Allende. These silhouetted figures against the setting sun create a dramatic image as they travel down the narrow, winding stone-paved streets. A subject like this remains etched in our memory, but the photograph gives us tangible shapes, colors and values that we can translate into a painting. Some artists prefer to work from memory, but a photograph, no matter how bad or how good, serves as a reminder of the actual experience and may provide the catalyst that could get your creative juices flowing.

Ilona Fellows

Gary Holman

Barbara McFarland

152

This Polaroid taken in Portovenere, Italy, has a strange but wonderful light pattern that appeared accidentally. This serendipitous happening gave a new reality to the scene. Polaroid photos and digital cameras provide an instant sketch or value study. These reference photos will freeze the patterns of constantly changing light and shadow. By taking several Polaroid photos, you will gain more time to paint on location, especially if time is limited or the weather is uncooperative.

Try taking several photographs of the same subject. By working from only one photographic source, you can become too dependent on the colors and shapes in that singular image. By using several photographs, editing out the parts that are unnecessary, and relying on your intuition, you probably will achieve a more pleasing composition.

## *Inspiration is everywhere*

When **June Young** left her hotel one morning, she photographed this beautiful Hawaiian woman making leis in the ideal early morning light. Later, in her studio, June painted a soft grayed-down background to complement the woman's skin tones, keeping a sharp edge between the background and the sunlight on the woman's shoulder. Along the top of the woman's hands and arms, June softened the edge by adding a thin, hot pink line followed by a thin line of yellow, and, in doing so, produced a strong sunlit glow.

June Young

# Using your photographs as a compositional tool

June Young has graciously shared the following information on using a camera as a compositional and editorial tool.

"Setting up a still life like this composition titled THREE LEMONS AND A TOMATO is one of my favorite things to do. The ideas for things to use in a still life almost always are triggered by an object that I see at a friend's home or in an antique shop. Strong light on the simplest of objects can inspire a still life. I found this silver basket in an antique shop and knew instantly how light coming through the basket would look. The surface of the inside of the basket has a wonderful reflective quality and, because of the shape, a painting was conceived. In order to get the best reference photo, I will often take photos exactly at the same angle but making the camera focus on a different object in the setup. Notice how the top reference photo focuses on the bottom reflections in the basket and the bottom reference photo focuses on the outside reflections of the basket. These photos were enlarged and lightened.

"The setup started with the tablecloth, three lemons, the basket and lemon leaves. I found I needed to carry the red color of the cloth into the basket, so the tomato was added. It was exactly what was needed and a painting was born. Next, I took several photos of the setup, turning it slightly, always looking for that special hit of light that would accent the objects in the best possible way. I now had all the references I needed to do a good painting. First, I started out with a very detailed drawing, which I used as my road map. As I drew, I was constantly working out in my mind any problems that I might encounter on my painting journey. When my drawing was finished, I had painted the whole painting in my mind. Now, the challenge was to make the real painting look like my vision of what it should be."

"As careful as I am with my drawing or road map of the painting, I never forget about my artistic license because I know that often when we get off the main road of our journey, exciting things can happen. Never lock yourself into a place where you leave no options to deviate from your photographic references. Keep your mind open for any changes you can make to improve your painting. Maybe you need to change a color, leave an object out, add more light to a spot or change the background. As long as you are painting the things you know and love, you will create a successful painting and not merely a translation of your photo (photographic) references."

THREE LEMONS AND A TOMATO, June Young

# Using your camera to compose and edit your subject

"I use my camera as a sketchbook; I find it a great tool for composing and editing a subject for painting. A camera with a zoom lens that can be used with either an automatic or manual setting is ideal. I usually use a manual setting when taking reference photos because I am most interested in back lighting. An automatic setting does not work well when photographing against the light.

"After choosing which photo I am going to use for my painting reference, I have it enlarged to 8" by 10" and lightened so I can see what is in the darkest areas of the photo. When I am working on the painting, I use both the original photo and the enlarged, lightened one as references. This enables me to paint dramatic light, but still maintain colorful shadows.

"As valuable as my camera is, I always bear in mind how the camera distorts images—it changes colors, angles and sizes of subjects. I make the necessary corrections when I am working on my drawings and painting the image."

# Consider mixing media

Watercolor is traditionally combined with a preliminary pencil drawing, but the finished painting is still considered a watercolor. Maybe it is time for you to stretch your creative boundaries and try mixing pastels, inks, colored pencils, gouache or collage into the equation.

There are times when you have tried everything to complete a glowing, transparent watercolor and your work still does not meet your expectations. Perhaps you are frustrated because your painting looks too tight and overworked. This is the time to give yourself permission to try any technique that will express your vision. Cultivate an attitude of adventure by mixing media. You may surprise yourself with the results. I guarantee you will have fun and, as with any trial and error approach, you will learn something new. Anything is possible because you make up the rules and the combinations. The following ideas go beyond transparent watercolor and involve

a wide range of materials and techniques that cannot be achieved by watercolor alone. Throw off your inhibitions and try something new.

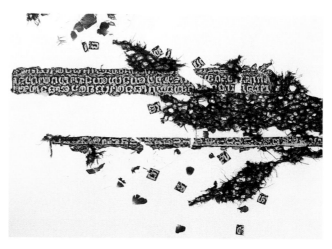

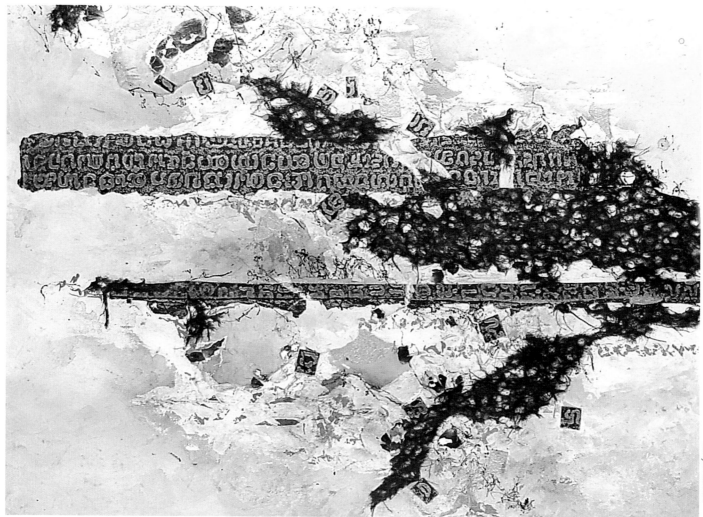

This image started with store-bought collage papers glued down with YES! paste. **Gel medium** was added to give the appearance of ancient, textured walls. This medium is thick and can be applied with a brush, knife or even a piece of cardboard, and can be thinned down to any consistency. Move the gel around on the surface of the paper to create textures. After the gel dries, color is applied and the paint will seek out the textural surfaces and create exciting relief shapes. The black lines are webbing spray.

# Breaking tradition— working dark to light using collage

Traditional watercolor is usually painted light to dark. Try reversing this sequence and let your emotions paint your picture. Sometimes you need to express yourself purely on a personal, emotional level and let your feelings drive the movement of the color on the surface of the paper. Choose a time when you can work spontaneously and let your feelings and intuition guide you. There is tremendous power in subjective painting. Using collage and experimenting with an abstract theme can help you unleash emotional expression not possible with traditional methods.

This collage painting breaks with tradition and involves working from darks to lights. When you work with collage paper, you can create beautiful darks instantly. Begin by playing with collage paper. Do not worry about a subject. Skip the drawing and value study and select colors that represent your feelings.

Using collage techniques will help you strengthen your sense of design. The best part about working with collage is that the work evolves quickly and gives you instant courage. You can literally play with the colors and move them around while you are orchestrating the design. An extensive variety of archival materials designed specifically for collage are available. Think about size relationships, values, movement and all the elements of design as you select your collage papers. Once you are pleased with your selection and arrangement of papers, glue them down. I prefer to use YES! paste because of its transparency and sticking power.

Karlyn Holman

# Mixing mixed-media

It is important to try as many media as possible to find which ones best suit your intent and your artistic personality. During your search, it is good to set goals and work towards accomplishing this aim, but always keep your antennae tuned in to a new direction. Keep an open mind and do not be afraid of trial and error. Know in your heart that your uniqueness will emerge. The following media are often combined with watercolor and can add an enriching surface to your artwork.

**Watercolor crayons**, like Caran D'Ache, are an exciting technical tool you can use to add enrichment and variety to your paintings. They can be drawn onto the wet paper or onto dry paper and wet later.

Karlyn Holman

**Gouache** is an opaque, water-soluble medium that is portable, fast-drying, and very similar to watercolor. This ancient opaque medium allows the light to reflect off the surface of your colors, rather than off the white of the paper. You can use the same brushes and the same painting ground as you would for watercolor. Gouache is a mixture of transparent watercolor and white paint. It may be purchased pre-mixed or you can make your own. Gouache is soluble, so when applying layers of color, be aware that you can lift up the undercolor. This quality can be an advantage when you want to soften an area or an edge. Gouache, like transparent watercolor, lightens when it dries, making it difficult to match a color later. Gouache is a natural choice for salvaging an "old dog" painting because you can cover up areas that you may be displeased with and regain the whites.

It Snowed in April, Jean Tori

**Jean Tori** painted this image, IT SNOWED IN APRIL, using gouache on handmade paper.

Karlyn Holman

**Colored inks** may be water-soluble or waterproof and are often made with dyes rather than pigments. Historically, dye-based inks were used for reproduction of commercially-produced artwork and longevity was not of prime importance. If you choose to use colored inks, research your choice so you select a brand with archival quality.

This painting was created in 1984 using permanent ink and was framed with regular glass. The image below shows how the same painting looks in 2002. Ink paintings should be framed using UV (ultraviolet) protective glass to prevent the ink from fading.

Karlyn Holman

# Fantasy on paper using gouache

## jean 2001

Jean Tori's art is a blend of her active imagination and her unique perspective, which she uses to interpret her life experiences. Jean uses vivid and graphic colors on precious papers that she lovingly prepares by hand. Her fantasy subjects are depicted in an expressive style, served up with color, wit and Asian symbolism.

"I developed my imagination and love of colour in my family's typical English country garden. My father grew prize-winning roses and dahlias, and it is a rare painting that does not contain some references to nature's floral handiwork. My chosen medium is and has always been gouache because it is thick, creamy and opaque and is so well suited for my vibrantly-coloured compositions.

BEACH TIGER, Jean Tori

ORIENTAL SHEEP, Jean Tori

RABBIT, Jean Tori

"My commercial design background and the years I have lived in Asia have been the biggest influences in my work. Korea introduced me to humor, style and colour through Korean folk art. I discovered the textures of Korean handmade paper and learned to make Korean screens. This skill is the basis for my paper ground. I glue together layers of handmade paper and then paint directly on this surface. I use a special Korean glue to form a strong and durable paper canvas. This process is slow and elaborate and can take up to ten days to complete. I am attracted to the nubbed and porous textures of the paper, which I feel is almost too beautiful to paint on, and I often have the paper around for weeks before I can take a paintbrush to the surface. The texture of the papers often offers suggestions as to the final subject of my painting."

Old Bali, Jean Tori

"I usually work with busy compositions; however, lately I have shifted towards minimalist works with only five or six colours. I live in Italy, but I love to incorporate Asian symbols and designs with the Italian countryside."

Teapot, Jean Tori

Along Umbrian Lines, Jean Tori

Umbrian Countryside, Jean Tori

CONSIDER MIXING MEDIA 163

# A passion for portraits

## JOHN MCFARLAND

John loves to draw and particularly enjoys working in colored pencils because he can draw and "paint" at the same time. He thoughtfully layers color over color, as he attempts to capture the many layers of a subject's persona.

"Most of my subjects are friends, relatives and family members. I usually take several photographs of my subject and then work from one or more of the photographic images. While colored pencil (Faber Castell-Polychromos) is my primary medium, silver point, watercolor and ink are also used, and recent works have incorporated the use of metallic paints and metal foils as well. The first step in the process involves capturing a good likeness. To accomplish this, I use a medium pink or an intermediate red, as either color blends well with the subsequent colors in developing skin tones. I use short, light strokes to capture the initial likeness and to clearly indicate areas of light and shadow. I then introduce additional light strokes of color, building up the deeper values through the application of many layers and the use of contrasting and complementary colors.

"I avoid any kind of direct pressure on the surface of the Winsor Newton 140# hot press paper and keep a very fine point on the pencils, allowing the irregularities of the paper to pull color from the pencil tip. While this method requires many passes to develop the depth of value desired, it also greatly facilitates blending and lifting color. To lift color from an area, I use an art gum eraser and, as many times as necessary, press the eraser onto the area to be corrected. During the lifting process, I am careful not to rub the eraser back and forth over the surface to avoid damaging the paper fibers."

THE DEER HUNTER, John McFarland

Jan, John McFarland

JAN. "This work in progress is my homage to Jan Hartley, who has led me to find places within myself I didn't know existed and to find a spiritual path that has provided me with rich and diverse artistic subject matter. I will forever be grateful to her for opening these doors for me, and I hope my portrait of her, when finished, will reflect the goodness and wisdom of this wonderful woman."

THE DEER HUNTER. "This portrait is of my stepfather, a wonderful human being, wise and good. He is a keen observer of wildlife and has spent most of his life pursuing his great love of the outdoors and hunting and fishing. His image in this painting is my vision of him, part Shaman, part deer hunter, part wise counselor—the wolf and raven as symbols of these aspects of his nature."

"When a portrait is successful, it is almost like bringing a person to life. This is the most gratifying and satisfying part of my art. These works are part of a series I am currently engaged in, reflecting my personal spiritual quest. With each persona, I try to describe symbols that I intuit to be associated with the person's life or with my perception of him or her as a person. These symbols are then incorporated into the work along with other imagery reflecting my quest to understand the physical world. I develop these symbols and images through a meditative process and, occasionally, from dream imagery. While this form of art is a very personal spiritual expression, it is my hope these images will have a more universal appeal and the symbolism will resonate with the viewer on multiple levels."

OUT OF AFRICA. "Gail is an Antiguan woman who left the islands early in her life and made her way to the United States, studying marine biology for a master's degree. She has come back to the islands to help her family and contribute to the development of the region. She is a very strong woman, possessing a powerful intellect, combined with a gentle and caring nature. I see her as a Nubian Queen, and my portrait of her incorporated some Egyptian symbols as well—I sense in her a very ancient spirit."

MISS JANIE. "Miss Janie was born with a deformed foot and lived her entire life on the island of Nevis, mostly in the small village of Cole Hill, in a one-room island house. In spite of her physical handicap and the hardships of her life, she was a towering figure, and seer for the locals, wise beyond words. We came to know her not long after we moved to the island, and in time, she called us her 'children.' She passed away two years ago, and I wanted to memorialize her with this work. The symbols are many, but the most significant are the raven (wisdom) and the salamanders (life and wisdom)."

# Creating multi-layers of interpretation

*Lana L Grow*

Lana engages the viewer by using rich, multi-layered surfaces. Layering color over color or material over material builds depth and luminosity. The richness of several layers interacting together and the sense of mystery created by successive layers peeking through her painting are the elements that make her work unique.

"I have always loved the flow and vibrancy of water media because the idea of the media working for me is intriguing. Finding ways to express my spirit in art has been a fun, exciting and sometimes exasperating experience. I have never really followed the rules because early on, I realized that what I really want to do is express my art in my own way. Experimenting and trying new ways to work in water media has kept me excited and enthusiastic about working as an artist. I have tried to find the medium that best fits my artistic temperament, and my inquisitive nature has helped me seek new ways to express my vision in my work. Knowing my natural tendencies and accepting myself as I am has made all the difference in my search.

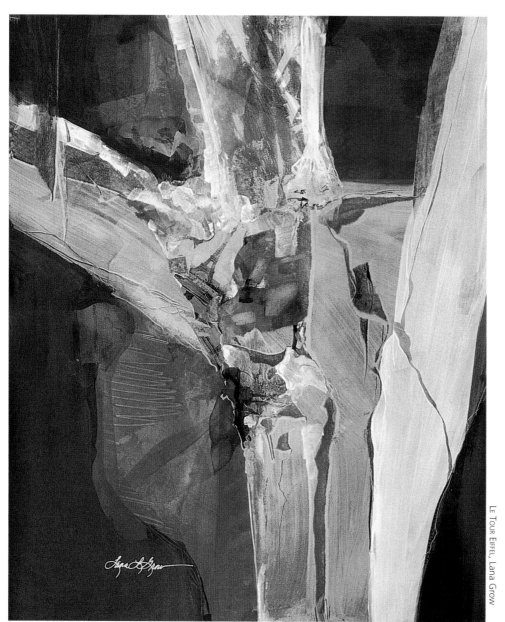

Le Tour Eiffel, Lana Grow

"Acrylic paint in water media is my latest passion. By using acrylic paint, I am able to layer, scrub, scratch, destroy and rebuild until the images begin to evolve and communicate a direction. I let myself go and give myself permission to experiment! I often work on several paintings at one time to keep my momentum going and my eye fresh. I use any thing I can think of to bring about a painting that will communicate an emotion, feeling or scene. The forgiving nature of acrylic combined with collage has given me the solutions I have needed to complete the language of my work. I have enjoyed building on the various media of my past experience and have combined them with new tools and techniques. Teaching and sharing my discoveries has been another step in my search for artistic expression and has provided an added bonus in my creative adventure.

"My process of painting LE TOUR EIFFEL began with several layers of transparent color. I allowed various layers to be revealed, first randomly, and finally, selectively. Opaque whites and collage papers were added for drama and mystery."

"My inspiration comes to me in many ways. Sometimes I have a particular memory or subject matter in mind, and other times I have nothing except color and shape. God's gifts to me are a constant inspiration. Most of all, I want to express the emotional involvement I feel about a place or moment. Inspiration could come from a rolling hillside, an experience during a trip to the tropics, a gorgeous sunset, or the peaceful beauty of water and pines trees. The intense colors of fall, the fresh greens of spring, and the world around me with its color and texture often show up in my work. I may be inspired by a powerful experience in nature, a beautiful scarf with colors that I love, or my observation of a wonderful piece of art. Any of these subjects may provide the springboard to my next painting or series. I focus on using colors I love, combined with line and texture, to help me bring about an arrangement of shapes and a pleasing design message."

SEE BEYOND HORSE AND MAN, Lana Grow

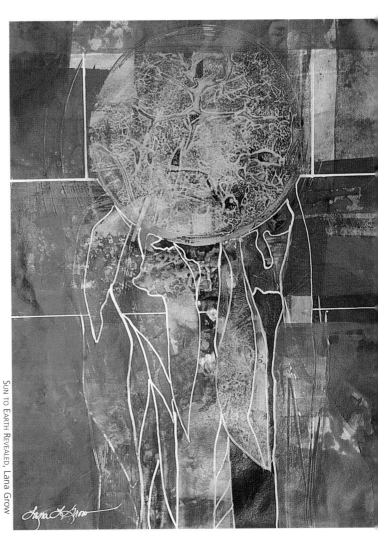

SUN TO EARTH REVEALED, Lana Grow

"SEE BEYOND HORSE AND MAN began with a series of transparent layering. Addition of opaque layers, collage pieces of a magazine photo, gold leaf, rice paper, cra-pas, metallic inks and skeleton leaf were incorporated to add character and depth to the texture of the surface. Each step inspired the next as I bonded with the surface.

"I began SUN TO EARTH REVEALED with an idea of expressing a round sun shape. I wanted to experiment with plastic, acrylic, water in layers and yellow (a color I rarely use). As the layering process progressed, I was careful to observe and capitalize on the areas of rich happenings and develop areas to complement this process by allowing the transparent areas to interchange with opaque rest areas. Adding line and definition completed the work."

"DANCE WITH THE EARTH'S LIMITATIONS began with several layers of transparent acrylic. As the painting evolved, the organic images suggested a forest dance. The use of black and white gesso in a frame-like format helped contain the emerging images. Adding a skeleton leaf, gold pen and layers of rice paper gave the piece texture, variety and order. This painting was an evolving dance using paint, texture, color and collage pieces."

"EMISSARY OF LIGHT AND FORM was created by isolating a design with a small frame. I used liquid acrylic in selected areas and left light areas that allow the viewer's eye to travel through the piece. Texture was added by experimenting with plastic and bubble wraps. By adding a dash of red in selective areas, I achieved the sense of mystery I was looking for."

"Painting is about new discoveries—-sharing, risking, being open to change, singing, experimenting, laughing at yourself and feeling open to the world around you. Painting can be an adventure of new revelations about yourself and the world of art. The process will build you up and, in the next moment, cut you down and keep you humble, but it can also teach you how to capture, with your craft, a work of art that expresses your personal vision and feelings. Your successes and failures during the process will fill you with the curiosity to continue. The journey is never boring and always a challenge."

# Mixing watercolor with pastels

Elsie works in many media and has found that starting her pastels with watercolor is an exciting combination to try when working with mixed-media.

*Elsie Cook*

"Watercolor and pastels mix beautifully and can be used together on many different kinds of paper, including watercolor paper and sanded papers that take wet medium. If you are painting on a dark background, I advise using opaque paint such as American Journey watercolors. Transparent watercolors work well on white or very light-colored paper.

"Because good, dark values are much harder to achieve using pastels, I begin by establishing dark values using my opaque watercolors. For added interest, try using complementary colors in your underpainting. I have found that using complementary colors adds a subtle glow to my skies and enriches my areas of shade.

"After my watercolor has dried, I begin building up layers of pastels, using harder pastels, such as Nupastels or Rembrants. Then I proceed with softer pastels, such as Sennelier, Schmincke or Unison. It is an exciting process to see the mixtures come alive!

"Pastels are also great for fixing up ruined watercolors because you can use them to paint directly over the areas that need improvement. Have fun discovering the different results you can achieve using a combination of watercolors and pastels."

Elsie Cook

"One need not go very far from home to find inspiration for one's work. One spring evening as I stepped out my front door, the birches by our driveway were backlit, casting wonderful shadows into the grass. To my surprise, a multitude of purple and white balloon flowers had appeared out of nowhere. Grabbing my camera, I took almost a whole roll of photos, including close-ups and distant shots, and I have used these photos many times since."

# Work on a variety of paper surfaces

Your choice of paper surfaces influences the character of your work. Investigating and trying new paper surfaces is one way to add excitement and variety to your search for personal expression.

**Cold Press paper** is probably the most popular choice of paper for most watercolor artists. This paper is internally sized and has a slightly toothed, forgiving surface which allows you to mask, erase easily and, most importantly, not reactivate underlying colors when they are rewet.

This on-location painting from Umbria, Italy, was painted on cold-pressed paper because of the need to layer color over color.

Karlyn Holman

**Yupo paper** is a man-made, synthetic paper. Yupo is made in Japan and, in the early 1980's, it was called Kimdura. The paint takes a long time to dry on Yupo paper because the surface is nonabsorbent and does not buckle when wet. Because the surface is plastic, it is not advisable to use a hair dryer to dry the paint. Yupo has become somewhat controversial because most watercolor societies prefer that artists work on an absorbent surface.

Karlyn Holman

**Masa paper** is an archival, very white Japanese paper that leaves batik-like cracks on the surface. During the process of working with this paper, you actually break the sizing into fractured patterns.

Karlyn Holman

**Coating paper with gesso** results in a surface similar to hot-pressed paper. Simply apply several coats of gesso onto any watercolor paper. In fact, this is a great way to recycle old dogs because the gesso completely covers any image that may be on the surface. Watercolor paint lies on top of the gesso and can be lifted easily. Use a very soft brush to layer color as the underlayer may reactivate with each successive layer you apply.

Karlyn Holman

# Capturing the soul

*Michaelin Otis*

DOÑA ISABEL, Michaelin Otis

"Discovering hot-pressed watercolor board was a real revelation for me. I have a severely handicapped son, and painting has provided a great escape for me. Because my free time was so limited, I always wanted to start painting immediately and did not want to take the time to stretch, staple or tape down my paper. I did not want to waste a second of my stolen moments on preparation. I started to try out different kinds of board surfaces and, when I tried a hot-pressed board, I fell in love. I was entranced as I watched the colors swirl and blend. Over the years, Crescent 115 has become my favorite surface.

"Backgrounds are usually the most difficult part of a composition for me. I have spent hours on a portrait only to ruin it by overworking the background. I learned to solve this problem two ways. Sometimes, I design the picture by doing a loose value study of darks and lights. Then, after a detailed drawing on the board, I paint the background first. That way, if I do not like the result, I can just try again without painting the subject. Sometimes, I do several backgrounds before finding one that I like well enough to paint the figure. I try and

get the look I want with the first washes, adding more color while the surface is still wet. Glazing color over color is difficult on hot-pressed board because you run the risk of lifting the first layer. This technique is possible, but you have to work quickly and your painting will never look as fresh as it did the first time.

"Doña Isabel was a model for me while I was teaching a workshop in Guatemala. I love older faces filled with wisdom, and she looked to me as if she knew all the secrets of life."

"The central figure in CULTURAL BLEND was blurred by softening the edges repeatedly with water after the painting had dried. This made the figure look out-of-focus and turned it into a design element instead of the center of interest. Even though this painting was not done wet-into-wet, the hot-pressed board allowed me to go back and soften edges long after they were dry.

CULTURAL BLEND, Michaelin Otis

IRIS WALTZ, Michaelin Otis

"Hot-pressed board worked especially well in IRIS WALTZ. My goal was to approach this realistic subject matter in an abstract manner. I wanted to lose some of the flowers in the wet-into-wet background, so again I painted the background first. Softening the edges of the background into some of the flowers was actually done before the flowers themselves were painted."

# Hot off the press

## Joyce Gow

Joyce maintains an uncanny balance between spontaneity and a strong sense of design, and she can capture any subject with only a few strokes of color. Her flair for semi-abstraction enriches these beautifully-executed artworks.

LEAFSCAPE #2, Joyce Gow

"Many years ago I purchased a full sheet of Arches 140# hot press paper. Over a year passed until I felt brave enough to try it. I was hooked! I love the way the colors dry on the smooth surface, glowing on the paper rather than being absorbed by the blotter-like action of cold press. This paper is not for those who like more control over washes. Hot press paper dries in arbitrary ways, leaving interesting marks and edges, which I personally prefer.

"The slick surface is ideal for lifting, scraping and knife painting. The spatula or knife glides across the paper smoothly. Salt also acts more aggressively, and I like the way the surface receives plastic wrap texturing. The crisp edges achieved with negative painting are lovely. "

WHITE PETUNIA BOUQUET, Joyce Gow

"I feel that hot press, plate, Bristol and illustration board offer many options. These papers have unique qualities that make them unpredictable. The smooth, dense surface has so little tooth that the color lies on top of the paper for quite awhile before absorbing into the surface. This quality gives me the advantage of charging in color wet-into-wet and moving it around. When the paint finally dries, I love how the color appears more intense and brilliant. The smoothness of the paper seems to enhance the luminosity of the colors.

"Lifting color is easier on smooth-surfaced paper because the paper resists absorbing the color. This means that when you glaze successive layers, you may lift the undercolor. This can be an advantage if you enjoy lifting color for special effects. The underlayer may be rewet and mingled with each new wash. Bleedbacks are a regular occurrence because of the uneven drying on the dense surface."

MAIN STREET, Joyce Gow

"This montage, MAIN STREET, was painted on location during an eight-day visit to Sneem, Ireland."

POINSETTIA #13, Joyce Gow

# Traditional painting on a nontraditional surface

In your continual search for new surfaces, try using this simple preparation to add visual excitement to your work. You can create a nontraditional surface by gluing a sheet of rice paper over an entire sheet of any watercolor paper. I prefer to use a highly fibered paper so the surface will provide surprises later. One of my favorite papers is Thai, white, fibered paper (10-gram weight). Place the rice paper, fibered side up, on top of the watercolor paper. For glue, use matte medium (or YES! paste) thinned with water and apply it directly on top of the rice paper. Saturate the paper in order to assure a good bond. To avoid air pockets and creases, begin gluing in the center of the paper and work towards the edges. Let these papers dry thoroughly before painting.

As you paint on this nontraditional surface, you will notice that colors will lift more easily. Additional layers of color should be applied with a soft brush so as not to disturb the underlying color. The added texture creates the illusion of a collage even though the painting was actually painted in a traditional way.

Karlyn Holman

This semi-abstract interpretation of petunias revealed many surprises as the color was applied over the unique surface. You must remain open to the unexpected and welcome serendipity.

Karlyn Holman

This painting of fuchsias was painted in several layers. First, a totally abstract nonobjective pattern of color was used to create the underpainting and the fuchsias were later painted on top of this design.

# Come back with a fresh eye

Karlyn Holman

*"Every now and then go away, have a little relaxation, for when you come back to your work your judgment will be surer; since to remain constantly at work will cause you to lose power of judgment."*
**Leonardo Da Vinci (1452-1519)**

Creating images is not always a smooth process from the beginning to the end. A great start can turn into frustration when your expectations do not match the reality of the painting. Whether you are trying to finish a painting, write a poem or even face a difficult situation, one of your best strategies is to take a break and come back with a fresh eye later. This break could last for months or years, but usually, it only takes the time necessary for a quick cup of coffee or a short walk. Knowing when to take a break from your work really helps you see what is necessary to resolve your painting. Knowing when to quit is one of the most difficult decisions you will have to make because there is no magic formula to inform you when your painting has had its final stroke. Working on more than one painting at a time and switching from painting to painting may keep your eye fresh and may give you ideas for resolving your work. Experience will teach you to trust your intuition and make the best decision.

There are several ways to objectively evaluate your paintings. One way is to observe your painting using an overhead mirror, thereby reversing the image. Some artists simply turn their paintings upside down and evaluate them. Using a reducing glass or looking through your camera lens will help you see your painting as a whole and not as many little parts.

# Keep an open mind

*"Inspiration far more often comes during the work than before it."*
**Madeleine L. Engle**

There will be times when you may feel totally uninspired. The creative process is not always continuous, and the execution of an idea can be interrupted or even roll to a stop. Keep an open mind because the process may still be incubating. Do not be discouraged and do not be afraid to change directions. This may be a time when embryos of ideas are forming below your consciousness. Do not demand perfection of yourself. This is a time to reflect, to journal and to try to visualize the direction you may want to go. Keep the faith that your uniqueness will eventually emerge. Connect with the artist within and cherish this time to dream!

Karlyn Holman

This painting had many lives before the final layers of paint revealed the image of calla lilies.

Karlyn Holman

I hope this book will help you find the images that are in your heart. Keep searching and growing and discovering!

# Conclusion

My journey through the world of watercolor is a continuing adventure and I still find myself learning and discovering every day. I hope the artwork and personal messages provided by the contributing artists will offer you immense inspiration. My personal hope is to share with you the joy and the passion that watercolor has brought into my life.

I have been fortunate to have had so many wonderful teachers, and the instruction I have received has been invaluable to my artistic development. In turn, I have attempted to offer you the basics of watercolor, plus share with you the many techniques I have experimented with and devised over the years. The creative energy generated through my association with other artists has provided stimulation and sustenance, but the main impetus for my search has come from within and there is still no end in sight.

As you continue along your journey, you will begin to fully understand the basics and think less and less about techniques and more and more about the vision you want to create. This is when the real effort of self-exploration begins. This is when you need your own space and time to explore and discover. Remember that your search is one with no end and no clear guidelines. Carry along with you your memories and life experiences because they form the inspiration that will keep you moving forward. By opening up your heart and soul to your search, you will soon discover the inexhaustible artistic possibilities within you.

While you are searching, growing and discovering personal fulfillment, be sure to enjoy the ride. The artist's search can be a series of fertile periods, dry spells, changes in direction, blocks and technical complications, but the search is worth the challenges. Making art is the result of working hard and never giving up. Each work, whether successful or unsuccessful, is a stepping-stone to your next work. Each stop and start is a catalyst for your growth as an artist. Let your work guide you in your search. Let your heart and hand, your strengths and weaknesses, and your hopes and dreams be your navigational tools to guide you on your journey. You may never reach your final destination, but my greatest hope for each of you is that you will laugh every day, have the courage to live your life with no regrets and never give up your dreams.

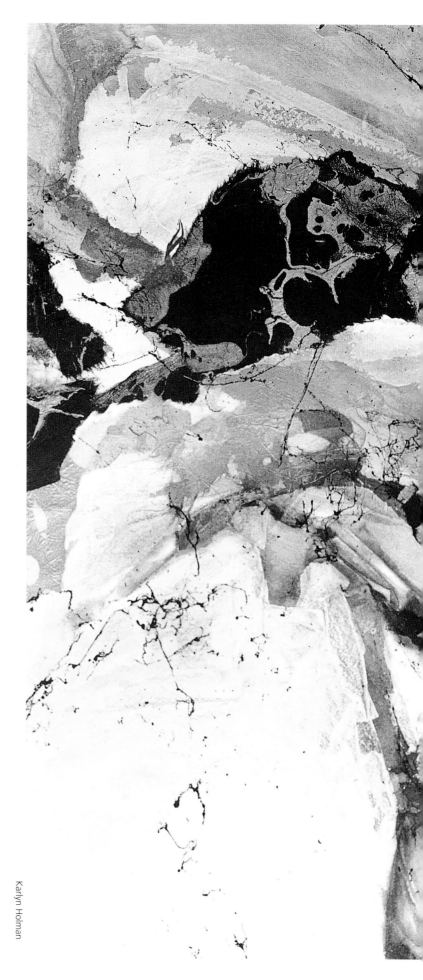

Karlyn Holman

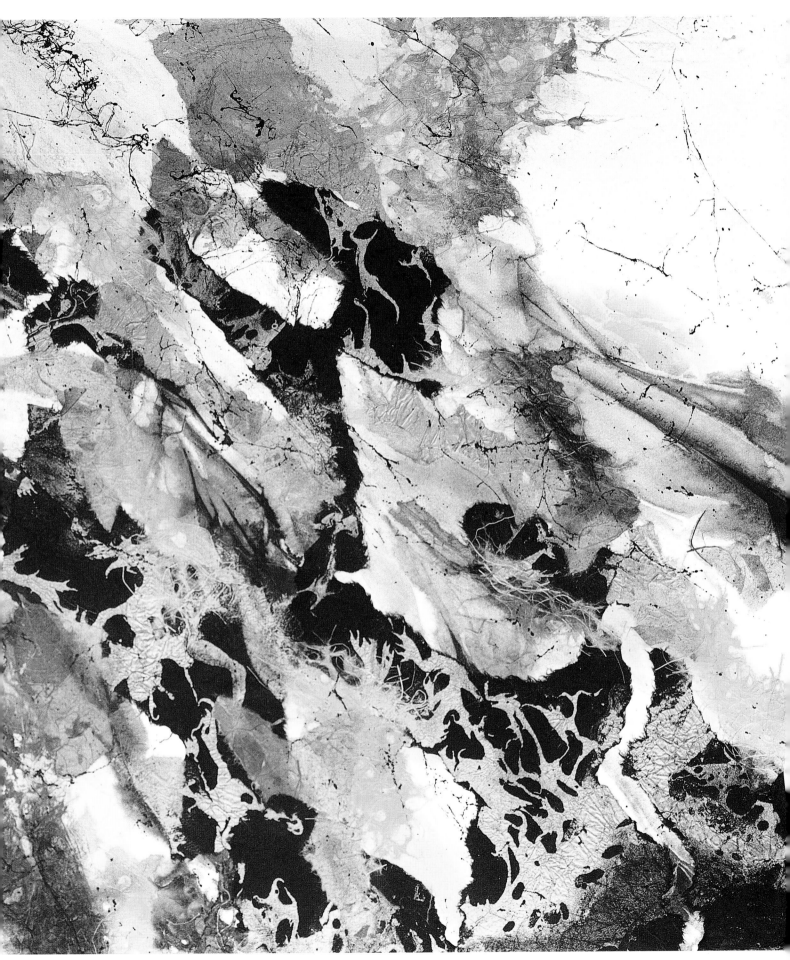

# Index of Contributing Artists

# Index

# Books and instructional videos by Karlyn

*Watercolor Fun and Free* is a 160-page book that has hands-on demonstrations and covers three major subject areas—abstraction, floral design and landscape design.

**Five-Day Workshop.** This six-hour video was recorded live during a five-day workshop. Subjects taught include abstract painting, portrait painting, wildflowers in a design, and capturing light on water lilies.

**Abstract Expression.** This four-hour video, recorded in Karlyn's studio, features the endless possibilities of approaching the abstract image, including collage techniques, free-flowing nonobjective painting, as well as approaching a subject in a semi-abstract presentation.

**The Landscape in Watercolor.** This four-hour video, recorded in Karlyn's studio, features how to capture light and mood, painting in many seasons, painting on location and a broad range of technical aspects of painting a landscape.

## Videos soon to be available:

**A Positive Approach to Negative Painting in Watercolor.** This video contains five step-by-step demonstrations to help you find success using a negative painting style. The demonstrations cover realistic, semi-abstract and nonobjective painting styles, and an intuitive style of painting by Bonnie Broitzman. This video runs for two hours.

**Floral Expression** and **Semi-Abstraction** are in the planning stage.

## Illustrated Children's Picture Books in hardcover:

*Christmas Song of the North*
by Marsha Bonicatto

*Little Brother Moose*
by James Kasperson

*Grandpa's Garden*
by Shea Darian

*Ditch of Witches*
by Warren Nelson

## Contact Information:

**Karlyn's Gallery**
318 West Bayfield St.
Washburn, WI 54891
Phone or Fax: 715.373.2922
E-mail: karlyn@karlynholman.com
Website: www.karlynholman.com

**Bayfield Street Publishing**
www.bayfieldstreet.com

184